Atlas of
Weapons and War

Illustrations by
Gerry Embleton

Maps by Geographical Projects London

Atlas of
Weapons and War

John Williams

The John Day Company New York

Geographical Director **Shirley Carpenter**
Editor **Maurice Chandler**
Art Director **Roger Hyde**
Research **Marian Berman**

Printed and bound in Spain

Library of Congress Cataloging in Publication Data
Williams, John, 1908 – 76
    Atlas of weapons and war.
    Includes index.
    1. Military art and science – History 2. Military history. I. Title.
U27.W46   355'.009   76-3515
ISBN 0-381-98291-2
D. L.: S. S. 522/76

Printed and bound in Spain - by TONSA San Sebastián and RONER Madrid

Contents

Introduction

ATLAS OF WEAPONS AND WAR describes how communities ranging from walled farming towns to world super-powers have waged war from prehistoric times to our own day.

In Chapter 1, which begins with the building of fortifications around ancient Jericho and ends with the fall of the Assyrian Empire, we see the evolution of the main principles of warfare and the main kinds of weapon that were to persist until the coming of gunpowder. Chapter 2 ranges over the Persian Wars, the Peloponnesian War, the campaigns of Alexander the Great, and the mighty conflict between Rome and Carthage, showing armies operating on an increasingly organized footing. In the third chapter Goths, Huns and Vandals gallop into Europe, compassing the downfall of Rome and ushering in the age of cavalry that was to dominate western warfare until the advent of the longbow and heavy plate armour.

Chapters 4, 5 and 6 are all gun-dominated. The first shows the impact of cannon on fort design, and the effect of arquebus and musket on field warfare. The second sees the concept of total war creeping into military thinking, and Europe's newly industrialized nations pouring guns and conscripted men into the Napoleonic Wars, the Austro-Prussian War and the Franco-Prussian War. The third leaves Europe for America and the Far East, where gun warfare took on new aspects and offered lessons that Europe was too arrogant or too blind to learn.

Chapters 7, 8 and 9 deal with the wars of our own century—Chapter 7 with the long stalemate of trench warfare from 1914 to 1918, which was ended only by increasing mechanization; Chapter 8 with the Second World War, in which mechanization prevailed throughout; and Chapter 9 with the mixture of highly sophisticated weapons and crude guerrilla fighting that has marked the limited but portentous wars of the last 30 years.

The lucid non-technical text is brilliantly illustrated with more than 100 pictures of the battles, the weapons and the military leaders of ancient and recently past times. Large full-colour maps set out the geographical background and strategy of major campaigns. Simple sketch plans show crucial stages in decisive battles.

1 Ancient Warfare

Warfare of the simplest kind may have begun as far back as the Old Stone Age, when men with stone axes or wooden clubs first did battle with a rival tribe for food or shelter, or perhaps to seize a few womenfolk to ensure the continuance of the tribe. In those prehistoric days when life was hard, brutal and short, and resources were pitifully scarce, every stranger was an enemy. As time went on, weapons became more varied and highly developed, fighting groups grew larger, tactics and strategy were introduced, military leaders emerged and the motives for warfare extended beyond the need for mere survival and day-to-day subsistence to the quest for wealth, power, territorial possessions and religious domination.

An important step in the evolution of warfare occurred between 7000 and 5000 B.C., when men in parts of western Asia ceased being roving hunters and undertook some sort of primitive agriculture that enabled them to settle in permanent dwellings. A people capable of tilling the ground was liable to be attacked by less provident or less able groups intent on seizing the fertile land and its produce. Here, then, were the beginnings of organized fighting on a larger scale than hitherto, with slings and stones, bows and arrows, and with a clear-cut economic motive—acquisition of food resources and living space.

But attack is not the only aspect of war. Equally significant is the other side of the coin—defence. And the importance of defence was clearly recognized by about 7000 B.C., when the people of ancient Jericho, near the Dead Sea, surrounded their ten-acre town with a tall, massive wall of undressed stone and a broad, deep moat—the earliest known example of military fortification.

Our first real knowledge of warfare, however, relates to a much later period, between 4000 and 3500 B.C., when the civilizations of Mesopotamia and Egypt were taking shape, the first based on the river valleys of the Euphrates and the Tigris, the

The beginnings of organized war reach back to around 7000 B.C., when the early inhabitants of Jericho surrounded their town with a massive wall, as a defence against nomads armed with slings and stones, bows and arrows.

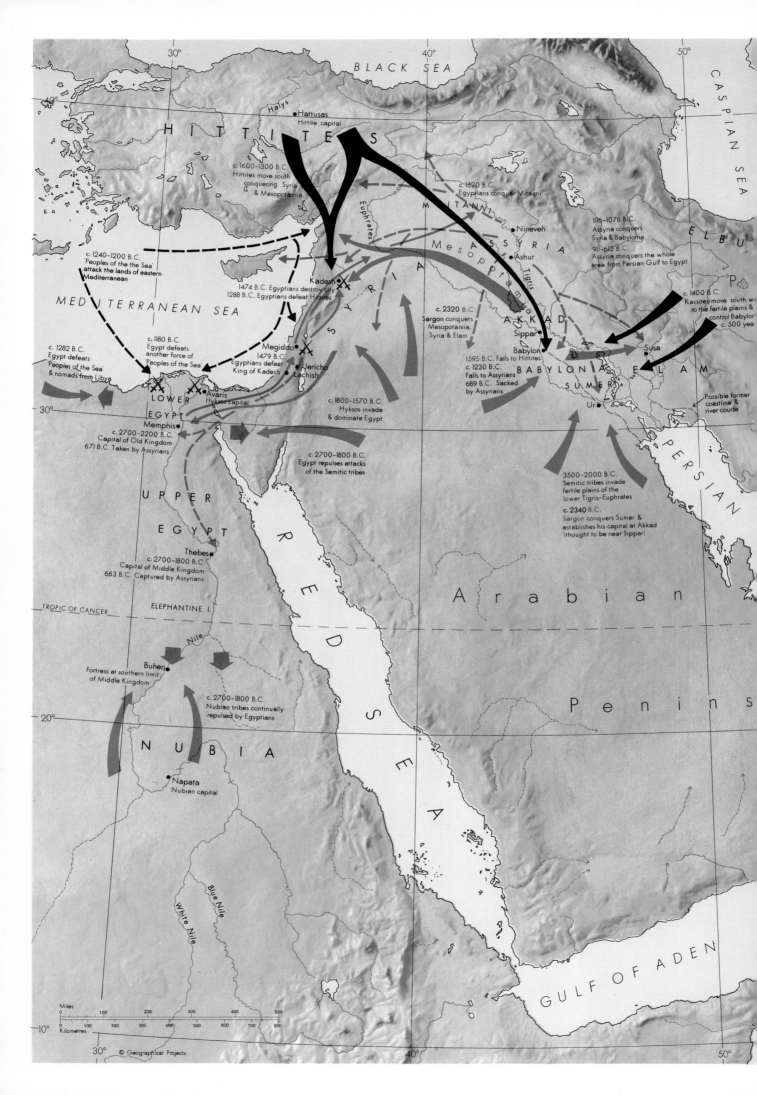

BLACK SEA

CASPIAN SEA

HITTITES

Halys

Hattusas
Hittite capital

c. 1600–1300 B.C.
Hittites move south
conquering Syria
& Mesopotamia

Euphrates

MITANNI

c. 1520 B.C.
Egyptians conquer Mitanni

ASSYRIA

Nineveh

Ashur

ELBU

1116–1078 B.C.
Assyria conquers
Syria & Babylonia

911–612 B.C.
Assyria conquers the whole
area from Persian Gulf to Egypt

c. 1240–1200 B.C.
'Peoples of the the Sea'
attack the lands of eastern
Mediterranean

Kadesh

1474 B.C. Egyptians destroy city
1288 B.C. Egyptians defeat Hittites

Mesopotamia

Tigris

AKKAD

c. 2320 B.C.
Sargon conquers
Mesopotamia,
Syria & Elam

P

c. 1400 B.C.
Kassites move south wi
to the fertile plains &
control Babylor
c. 500 yea

MEDITERRANEAN SEA

Sippar

Susa

ELAM

c. 1282 B.C.
Egypt defeats
'Peoples of the Sea'
& nomads from Libya

c. 1180 B.C.
Egypt defeats
another force of
'Peoples of the Sea'

Megiddo

1479 B.C.
Egyptians defeat
King of Kadesh

Jericho
Lachish

SYRIA

c. 1800–1570 B.C.
Hyksos invade
& dominate Egypt

1595 B.C. Falls to Hittites
c. 1230 B.C.
Falls to Assyrians
689 B.C. Sacked
by Assyrians

Babylon

BABYLONIA

SUMER

ELAM

Possible former
coastline &
river course

LOWER

Avaris
Hyksos capital

EGYPT

Memphis

c. 2700–2200 B.C.
Capital of Old Kingdom
671 B.C. Taken by Assyrians

c. 2700–1800 B.C.
Egypt repulses attacks
of the Semitic tribes

30°

Ur

3500–2000 B.C.
Semitic tribes invade
fertile plains of the
lower Tigris–Euphrates

c. 2340 B.C.
Sargon conquers Sumer &
establishes his capital at Akkad
(thought to be near Sippar)

PERSIAN

UPPER

EGYPT

RED

Arabian

Thebes

c. 2700–1800 B.C.
Capital of Middle Kingdom
663 B.C. Captured by Assyrians

TROPIC OF CANCER

ELEPHANTINE I.

Nile

Peninsula

Buhen

Fortress at southern limit
of Middle Kingdom

c. 2700–1800 B.C.
Nubian tribes continually
repulsed by Egyptians

20°

NUBIA

SEA

Napata
Nubian capital

Blue Nile

White Nile

GULF OF ADEN

Miles
0   100   200   300   400   500

Kilometres
0   100 200 300 400 500 600 700 800

© Geographical Projects

30°

40°

50°

10°

20°

30°

second on the valley of the Nile. These relatively small areas of fertile territory, surrounded by vast tracts of desert, were the scenes of constant warfare. They were fought for by both the local populations competing for living space among themselves and outside invaders from the desert lands seeking a more favourable habitat. And we know that the Sumerians, the first civilized people of southern Mesopotamia, were already putting warfare on an organized footing, for a Sumerian sculpture of the time portrays soldiers fighting in close order, carrying spears and shields.

The centuries that followed were a time of great military activity in both Mesopotamia and Egypt. Indeed, the period between about 3500 and 2000 B.C. saw the evolution of the main principles of warfare and the main kinds of weapons that were to persist until the introduction of gunpowder in the fourteenth century A.D. In this period came the first great historical struggle—between Sumerians and Semites—for the possession of Mesopotamia; and from that struggle emerged the famous Semitic leader Sargon.

Sargon conquered Sumer, and other fertile areas of Mesopotamia to the north of it, at some time around 2340 B.C. He went on to invade Syria and Palestine and spent some years subduing the "countries of the west," uniting them with Babylonia into a single empire and founding the powerful Akkadian dynasty. His troops, armed mainly with the javelin and the spear, also brought the chariot into battle.

The chariot—at this time drawn by four asses—was an epoch-making innovation. Its appearance in Mesopotamia, some time around 3000 B.C., marked the greatest military advance of this period. It introduced into fighting a mobility and flexibility unknown before. With two or four solid wooden wheels, each made of several sections, it carried a driver and a single soldier armed with spear and javelin. A line of chariots would charge the enemy to create panic and disorder, while close behind them the shield-protected infantry would follow, wielding their spears. Over the centuries the chariot was improved by various modifications: lighter bodywork, the replacement of heavy solid wheels by light spoked wheels, axles placed farther to the rear for better balance and greater manoeuvrability. These improvements allowed it to be used not only for charging the enemy but also as a stable platform from which a bowman could shoot accurately. But it was not until around 2000 B.C. that asses were replaced by horses, introduced into Mesopotamia from the north, thus making chariots far swifter.

The 1000 years and more of chariot development also witnessed improvements in other weapons of the ancient world. The mace started as a heavy stone head with a hole bored through it, into which a stout wooden handle was fixed. The Egyptians,

These lands that nurtured the first civilizations were also the first theatres of war. The map shows main events from about 3500 B.C., when Semitic tribes arrived in southern Mesopotamia, to 612 B.C., when the great Assyrian Empire was finally overthrown. Egypt's campaigns in Asia (thin blue lines) gave rise to the earliest battles to be recorded in detail—at Megiddo in 1479 B.C. and Kadesh in 1288 B.C.

who made it their main weapon for many centuries, experimented with heads of different shapes, including a pear shape, which was very effective for stunning an adversary, and a saucer shape, which was less effective for stunning but could wound an enemy to a limited extent. The saucer shape was fairly soon discontinued, presumably because inflicting a slight wound on an enemy was less desirable than cracking his skull. But gradually, in both Mesopotamia and Egypt, copper came into wider use. At first some of this new and still-precious material was used for making mace-heads, but a more important result was that metalworkers could now produce blades with a really sharp piercing or cutting edge, and soon a new weapon—the metal axe—made its appearance. Troops then had to be protected with metal helmets and capes studded with metal discs. Men so protected were no longer particularly vulnerable to mace blows, so by about 2500 B.C. maces had almost disappeared while the use of the axe had become more and more widespread.

In Mesopotamia axe-heads—first of copper, later of bronze—were socketed to take a handle and narrow-bladed for piercing; in Egypt they were simply bound to a handle and broad-bladed for cutting.

While metalworking remained in its infancy, men could successfully shape the comparatively small blades needed for axes, but they found it much harder to fashion the larger blades needed for effective swords. The first copper swords were therefore short, straight, dagger-like blades, usually nailed to a wooden handle and used for stabbing; but by the time of King Sargon, Mesopotamian soldiers were also beginning to use sickle-shaped swords for slashing. Yet the sword was not to become a vital factor in warfare until well after 2000 B.C., when bronze was replacing copper, and larger, sturdier blades could be produced. Meanwhile, between 3000 and 2000 B.C., the spear and the javelin were of far greater importance, especially in Mesopotamia. The long, thrusting spear, with its wooden handle and its socketed leaf-shaped blade, was the prime weapon of the infantryman. Javelins, of similar construction but considerably smaller, were the hand-hurled missiles of the charioteer, who commonly carried five or six of them in a quiver, as well as a spear, when he rode into battle.

Of longer range than the javelin was the bow, which was originally a hunting weapon in prehistoric times. Stone carvings made at the very dawn of history show that the Mesopotamian bow was the single-arc type, while the Egyptian one had a double-convex shape. As the centuries passed, the bow-string was brought under greater tension to increase the range, first by making the body of two strips of wood tightly bound together (the compound bow) and later by making it of several strips of different woods, backed by bands of sinew and strengthened on the

side nearest the string with animal horn (the composite bow). Yet, strangely, the bow played little part in Egyptian warfare until perhaps as late as 2400 B.C., and the Sumerians of southern Mesopotamia never used it at all. But the Semites exploited it to the full, and many archaeologists believe that it was the use of composite bows that enabled Sargon to win control of Mesopotamia and establish the Akkadian Empire.

In many respects the Egyptians lagged behind the peoples of Mesopotamia in weapons and methods of warfare. Long relying on the mace, the Egyptians were slower to introduce slashing and piercing weapons, slower to wear armour, and far slower to begin chariot warfare. Yet they created one of the greatest and longest lasting of all civilizations, destined to endure for nearly 3,000 years. During two long periods of their history—the Old Kingdom (about 2700–2200 B.C.) and the Middle Kingdom (2100–1800 B.C.)—most of the wars they fought were within their own borders or against Nubian and Semitic attackers from the south and east. In these wars Egypt's irregular troops generally acquitted themselves well, not only when fighting over open ground but also when building and defending their immense fortresses in Nubia, such as that at Buhen. But towards the close of the Middle Kingdom there came a period of peace and security during which preparedness for war lapsed. Egypt paid a high penalty. A century of rivalry for the throne ensued; then came an invasion by the Hyksos, or "Shepherd Kings," from Syria. Equipped with horse-drawn chariots and scimitars, the warlike Hyksos swiftly conquered Egypt, establishing garrisons and fortresses throughout much of the country. Their domination lasted for some two centuries until finally, about 1570 B.C., they were driven out by King Ahmose I, the first pharaoh of the New Kingdom, or Empire, period (about 1570–1100 B.C.).

Under Ahmose, Egypt became a military state, with an army its dominant feature. In contrast to the militia maintained in previous times, this was a standing army, organized in two great

Left: By about 2500 B.C. the axe had replaced the mace, and soldiers began wearing helmets. The Sumerian axe at the extreme left, with its narrow blade socketed to hold the handle firmly, was capable of piercing a metal helmet. The Egyptian axe of about 2000 B.C. (centre) was also socketed but, with its broad, curved blade, it was better at slashing than at piercing.
The last axe, of about 1450 B.C., had its head bound to the handle with leather thongs. This type of axe, more typical of Egypt, appears in the New Kingdom relief at the top of the page.

Right: Short-bladed Mesopotamian sword of about 2500 B.C., used for stabbing; Egyptian bronze sword-dagger of about 1800 B.C., strengthened with a rib to increase its power of penetration; sickle-like Egyptian sword of about 1300 B.C.—a slashing weapon.

"divisions," one in the Delta and one in the south. And it was with this army that, thanks to the experience gained in campaigns against the Hyksos, strategy and tactics first became an established part of military science as commanders began to think in terms of lines of battle, wings and centre, and flanking movements as well as frontal attack.

The new-style Egyptian infantry made increasing use of the battle-axe—now of the socketed type as used in Mesopotamia—to supplement the spear. Archers gave a new significance to the bow by shooting not raggedly but by volleys, a form of attack that made the Egyptian bowmen dreaded adversaries and brought them a reputation that lasted even into classical times. In addition there was an innovation for which Egypt had to thank its Hyksos conquerors—the horse. Although no cavalry in the modern sense was yet used, horse-drawn chariotry now became an important element of the Egyptian army, and the making of light, manoeuvrable chariots a growing skilled industry. Chariot divisions and infantry were trained to work in conjunction, with archers lending close support.

The struggle against the Hyksos had produced other advances too. Coded torch signals were introduced, messages were carried by runners, and orders were blared out by trumpet call. To supply intelligence, prisoners were taken and interrogated, while reconnaissance units were deployed and rear formations were constantly fed with reports from the front. The beginnings of an administrative system were now seen, and, along with a medical service, there were specialized bodies such as engineers, and transport units to convey heavy equipment such as siege apparatus.

The story of Egypt after Ahmose is one of continued war and conquest. His successor, Amenhotep I, having brought Nubia and Libya under control, marched northeast through Syria to reach the Euphrates. Amenhotep's son Thutmosis I, pushing still farther, conquered the people of Mitanni, northwest of Nineveh. Then, when he returned to Egypt, the Egyptian grip

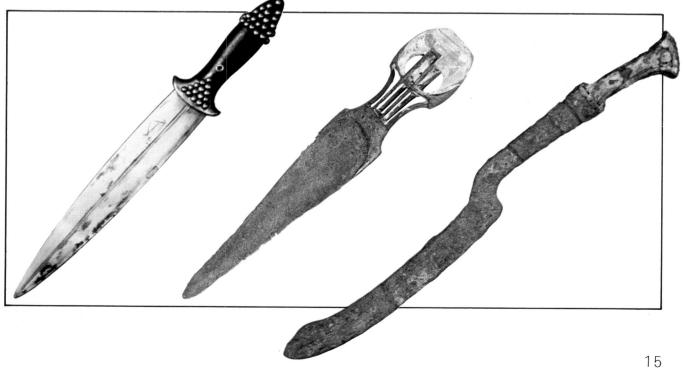

on the conquered lands weakened, and his son, Thutmosis III, had to deal with a revolt by the King of Kadesh, in Syria.

After a victorious battle at Megiddo in Palestine in 1479 B.C.—the first battle of which detailed accounts still exist—Thutmosis advanced to Kadesh itself; but although he sacked the city, the king escaped. After occupying the Phoenician coast, however, Thutmosis attacked Kadesh again a few years later, and this time victory was complete. After a long siege, Kadesh fell and the king's power was finally broken. Thutmosis went on to win further victories, and by the time he died in 1447 B.C. Egypt's imperial power had been fully restored.

For much of the next 150 years this power was under some strain, threatened by attacks from the Aramaeans as well as the Hittites of Asia Minor. By the end of this time, however, the Egyptian army was recovering its strength, and Ramses II, who came to the throne in 1292 B.C., decided to retrieve Egypt's losses by confronting the Hittites in their most southerly stronghold—Kadesh once again.

In the long years since Amenhotep's time, there had been considerable changes and developments in weapons. The sword—

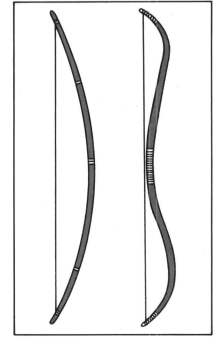

long as well as short—was replacing the axe and was commonly used by infantrymen fighting in close-ranked phalanx-like formation. (The phalanx proper—the arrangement of heavy-armed infantry into a tight body of spearmen—was a later Greek invention.) Equally important was the spear, used for defence of fortified positions as well as for attack.

But the master weapon was now the composite bow, with its reed-shafted, bronze-headed arrows, sufficiently powerful to penetrate armour at short range. The bow was used by infantrymen and charioteers alike. The charioteer's other weapon was the javelin, hurled from massed charges of perhaps as many as 50 vehicles together. The chariot was, indeed, becoming an increasingly vital arm for the Egyptians. Swift and manoeuvrable, drawn by two horses, it provided the great advantage of mobility. The earlier light model had now been followed by one of heavier design, and depots had been set up for chariot repair and maintenance.

Unlike Mesopotamian troops, Egyptian soldiers had not begun to use armour until as late as 1570 B.C. Previously the large shield was the soldier's only protection, but now charioteers and archers, who had no hand free to carry a shield, were provided with coats of mail or other material and helmets. The archer can be pictured as wearing a helmet of padded felt-like material, leather, or metal and a thick corselet of plaited flax cemented with glue. The composite bow he carried was double curved, and strapped behind him was his quiver of up to 30 arrows. The charioteer wore a similar helmet and a coat of bronze scales. The spearman, less likely to be armoured, carried a round-topped shield, three feet (nearly one metre) long.

Behind this fighting army a well-organized administrative "tail" was developing. Records of pay, equipment and so forth were being kept, and there were services for the distribution and transport of supplies. So in 1288 B.C., with what was now a formidable military machine, Ramses II prepared to face the powerful Hittite forces at Kadesh, on the river Orontes (Asi), just south of Lake Homs in Syria. This battle, like the earlier conflict at Megiddo, was to be one of the few of ancient times that can now be followed in detail from contemporary records.

Having divided his army of some 20,000 men into four divisions, south of Kadesh, Ramses led one of them northwards to the west of the city. The Hittites, under their general, Mutallu, thereupon advanced from north of Kadesh and skilfully moved in on Ramses from the southeast, isolating him from his other divisions, still some way south. Next, with chariots and infantry, the Hittites attacked the second Egyptian division as it approached Kadesh, cutting it to pieces. Part of this broken group fled north to where Ramses and Amon had already camped. The Hittites, in hot pursuit, overran the encampment and scattered the Egyptians. Ramses then managed to throw a chariot counter-attack against the Hittite eastern flank near the river.

Instead of maintaining the assault, the Hittite centre started looting the Egyptian camp, thus throwing away their chance of victory. For they were now attacked from the west by Ramses'

Above left: This wooden model, carved some 4000 years ago, shows Egyptian archers marching four abreast into battle. Real-life Egyptian archers of that time probably used bows made of acacia wood and arrows made of reeds. Left: The single-arc bow, favoured in Mesopotamia, and the double-convex bow commonly used in Egypt. Composite bows could be of either shape, but it was the composite double-convex bow perfected in Egypt that achieved the greater effective range.

17

crack Canaanite mercenaries and destroyed. Meanwhile, Ramses' charioteers and bowmen continued their push on the eastern flank, forcing the enemy back across the Orontes. Darkness was now falling, and with Ramses' third division advancing nearby to pose a new threat, Mutallu withdrew his troops into Kadesh. A siege might have followed, but instead Ramses retired too, without further action, and the battle ended indecisively. A peace pact was then made. It had been a close call for the Egyptians, but Ramses' leadership had saved the day.

Not long afterwards the power of both Hittites and Egyptians began to wane. New forces were arising to conquer and dominate these war-scarred lands. First came the migratory tribes from the Aegean region, who by 1200 B.C. had occupied the Hittite territories, had penetrated Syria, and were even threatening Egypt. The Egyptians, under Ramses III (1198–1167 B.C.), saved themselves from actual invasion by defeating the Aegean forces on the Phoenician (eastern Mediterranean) coast. But a few centuries later a more formidable aggressor was on the warpath— Assyria.

The Assyrians, inhabiting arid lands on the upper Tigris, were the most warlike nation of ancient times. Throughout three centuries of almost constant campaigning, beginning in 911 B.C., they won victory after victory, subjugating peoples to the north, west, east, and south and founding an empire that eventually stretched from the Mediterranean to the Persian Gulf and from

Three stages in the Battle of Kadesh, where an Egyptian army commanded by Ramses II clashed with a Hittite army led by Mutallu. For each stage of the battle, brief numbered paragraphs show the sequence of events. Stage 1, drawn to a smaller scale than stages 2 and 3, shows the line of Ramses' advance on the Hittite stronghold. At stage 2 it seemed that the Egyptians were facing certain defeat. But the arrival of Ramses' Canaanite mercenaries (stage 3) saved the day, and the battle ended indecisively. It was quickly followed by a peace pact.

Ramses II and his bodyguard
Egyptian divisions
Canaanite mercenaries
Hittite troops
Hittite chariots

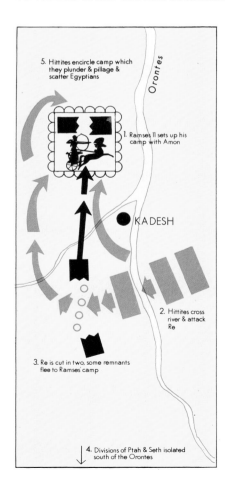

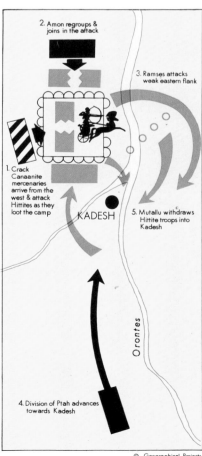

© Geographical Projects

Top of page: Relief showing an Assyrian
siege engine at the siege of Lachish
(700 B.C.). Missiles hurled from the
city wall by its defenders are raining
down on the engine. Above: Assyrian
slingers, trained to hurl heavy stones
with deadly accuracy at long range.

the former Hittite kingdom to Egypt (which they conquered in
671 B.C.). They fought for loot and sheer love of conquest, under
warrior kings, many of whose names were to become household
words in the history of war—Assurnasirpal, Tiglath-Pileser,
Sennacherib, Assurbanipal. Their empire lasted until 612 B.C.
when Nineveh, their capital, fell to a combined assault by
Scythians, Medes and Babylonians.

There were many reasons for the Assyrians' success in war.
Their rulers were mostly outstanding commanders; their military organization was good; they had a regular, well-trained
army; they pioneered the use of iron weapons (an advantage in
strength and durability) and of cavalry; they employed new,
imaginative tactics; they brought the bow, employed by mail-
coated archers, to a high pitch of effectiveness and similarly improved the chariot as an assault vehicle, increasing its crew first
to three, then to four. And they introduced a formidable new
weapon—an accurate sling. Above all, perhaps, they developed
siege craft, making full use of heavy but easily transportable siege
towers, battering rams, and hand-propelled armoured vehicles.

With the fall of the Assyrians the era of ancient warfare came
virtually to an end. During this epoch, there had been wars in
India and China too, but it was in the Near and Middle East that
warfare had become most highly developed. In the era that
followed, the scene was to shift largely westwards, to the warring
nations of Greece and Rome; and there naval warfare was soon
to play an important part.

2 Organized Warfare

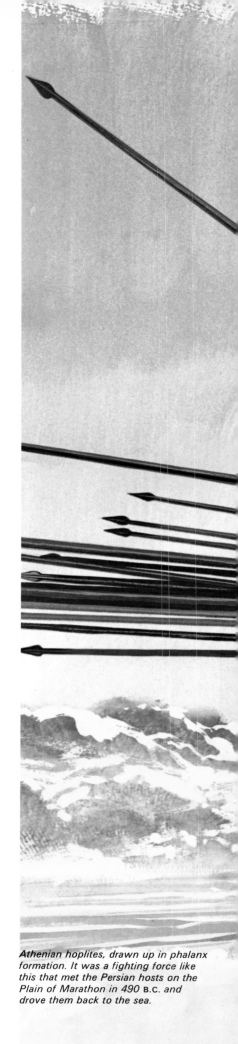

In the era of ancient warfare, ingenuity had shown itself mainly in establishing and improving the basic weapons of land fighting. In the following nine centuries, from 600 B.C. to A.D. 300, it was to show itself not only in further improvements of such weapons but also in the building and deployment of fighting ships, the evolution of new battle techniques and the upsurge of a class of men who made warfare their profession. And as the main theatre of war shifted from the Near East to the Mediterranean lands, this new class of professionals produced men such as Alexander the Great, Hannibal, Scipio Africanus and Julius Caesar—perhaps the world's first military geniuses.

By 539 B.C., less than 80 years after the Medes, Scythians and Babylonians had overthrown Assyria, they, in turn, had all been conquered by the Persians, then under the leadership of Cyrus the Great. During the next 40 years, with a formidable army of light and heavy infantry, charioteers and archers, backed by specialist troops employing camels and elephants, Persia continued her career of conquest and built up an empire that stretched from the edge of India to the coast of Asia Minor. Large-scale organized warfare made its first appearance in Europe early in the fifth century B.C., when the Persian king Darius I sent a powerful force across the Aegean to invade the Greek mainland. In 490 B.C. one small city state alone—Athens— was left to repel an attack by the greatest empire the world had yet seen; and at the Battle of Marathon, Athens succeeded.

During several centuries of intermittent local wars with other Greek states, Athens had perfected the phalanx—a massed formation of soldiers called *hoplites*, many ranks deep and standing shoulder to shoulder. The hoplite who made the long march from Athens to the Plain of Marathon, where the Persians had disembarked, was a formidable foe. Protected with a huge round shield, bronze helmet and cuirass and leather greaves covered with metal

Athenian hoplites, drawn up in phalanx formation. It was a fighting force like this that met the Persian hosts on the Plain of Marathon in 490 B.C. and drove them back to the sea.

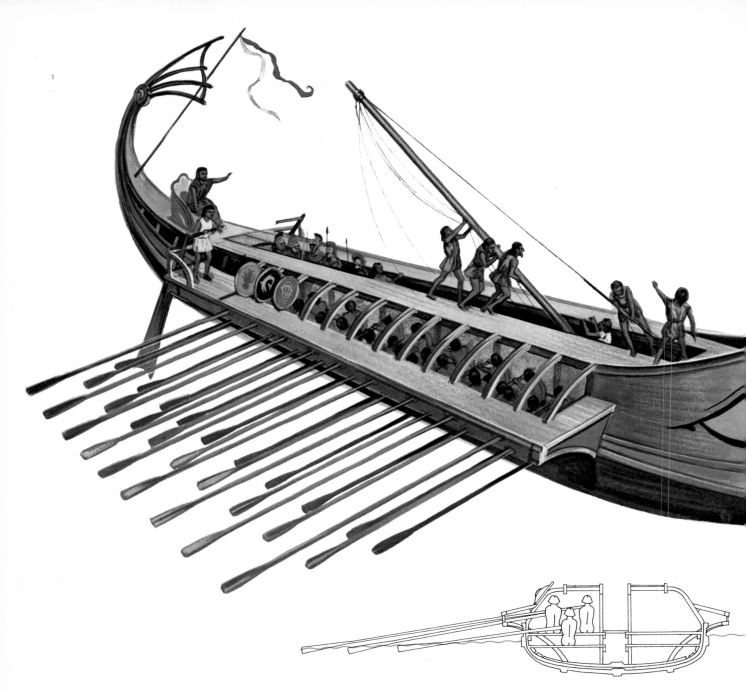

plates, he carried a short cut-and-thrust sword and a long spear. And moving forward shoulder to shoulder with his comrades in the phalanx, he repelled the far more numerous Persian troops and drove them back to their ships, to return home beaten.

As employed in wars between rival Greek states, the phalanx was designed to meet the enemy, drawn up in his own phalanx, head-on. The opposing sides would clash and stand their ground, fighting it out with spear and sword, men in the rear ranks stepping forward to fill the places of those who fell in front. Cohesion and discipline were everything: no gaps must be left, and the fight must go on until one side or the other broke and fled. In fact the phalanx battle was commonly a somewhat primitive slogging match. Perhaps it succeeded against the seasoned Persian troops mainly because it was new to them. In Asia the Persians were used to fighting on vast battlefields where there was ample space for the deployment of cavalry. At Marathon they were restricted to a confined space between the sea and high ground, and facing a solid wall of armed men, with little room to manoeuvre.

Reconstruction of a Greek trireme, and cross-section diagram showing how its three tiers of oarsmen were accommodated. When a trireme went into action its sail was lowered so that its course would not be affected by a change of wind. Its projecting metal-reinforced bows could shear off the oars of an enemy vessel or hole its hull. In close-quarter fighting the trireme's oarsmen could be protected by shields hung over the openings near where they sat.

Above: Map showing the great distances covered and the vast territories gained during Alexander the Great's campaign against the Persians. The broken black boundary line marks the extent of the Persian Empire around 500 B.C. The full black line marks the boundary of the empire Alexander won. Alexander began his campaign early in 334 B.C. By the end of 332 B.C. he had gained his main objective—to drive the Persians out of the eastern Mediterranean. Six years later he was in India, where he won his last great victory at the Hydaspes, an east-bank tributary of the Indus.

the Greek world under his control. His triumph was clinched at the Battle of Chaeronea in 338 B.C.—a battle in which his 18-year-old son Alexander led a brilliantly successful cavalry charge. Philip, not content with his already remarkable success, then went on to plan an attack on the Persian Empire, and only his assassination in 336 B.C. prevented him from putting the plan into effect. But Alexander, who succeeded him as master of Greece and Macedonia, wasted no time in doing so.

On his accession at the age of 20, Alexander found himself in command of what has been described as the most powerful and best-balanced army in the ancient world. It combined the rock-like steadiness of the phalanx with the speed and mobility of light and heavy cavalry. The main infantry, or phalanx, troops consisted of six or seven battalions, each of some 1,530 men, armed with a new 14-foot (3.3-metre) pike (the *sarissa*), instead of the shorter spear, and carrying a shorter shield than earlier Greek infantrymen. In addition there were three 1,000-strong battalions of *hypaspists*—crack infantrymen armed like the hoplites but more mobile—whose main role was to form a junction between phalanx and cavalry. The latter comprised eight squadrons of up to 300 horsemen each, equipped with a cuirass and a short, thrusting spear. These were all Greek troops. Supplementing them were units of heavy cavalry, lancers, archers, and javelin-men drawn from subject races. Finally there was a variety of siege equipment, ranging from towers and battering rams to incendiary mixtures and catapults.

Early in 334 B.C., Alexander crossed the Hellespont with some 34,000 infantry and 3,000 cavalry, determined to punish Persia for its earlier attacks on Greece and to seize its vast empire. The Persian forces ranged against him, though no longer as formidable as in their empire-building days, were vastly stronger numerically than his and, fighting on their home ground, were never faced with his problem of maintaining ever-lengthening supply lines. Furthermore, because the Persians held the Syrian coast, they controlled the sea approaches to their empire. Yet within three years Alexander had wrested all Persia's east Mediterranean ports from her, including the strongly defended island city of Tyre, which he captured by one of the most famous sieges in history. He had also sealed the fate of the Persian Empire by winning three great battles: at the river Granicus, in Asia Minor, in 334 B.C.; at Issus, near the northeast corner of the Mediterranean, in 333 B.C.; and at Gaugamela, to the east of Nineveh, in 331 B.C. Five years later he won his last major victory, east of the Indus, at the Battle of Hydaspes. Only then did his army refuse to go farther. Alexander had pushed his conquest to its logical limits.

Alexander's military genius showed itself in many ways: in the care he lavished on his troops; in his organization of a supply system that could keep an army at full efficiency half a continent from home; in the importance he placed on staff work and administration; and in the use he made of specialists in surveying, engineering and a score of other fields, including naval matters. His insistence on seizing Persia's Mediterranean ports before

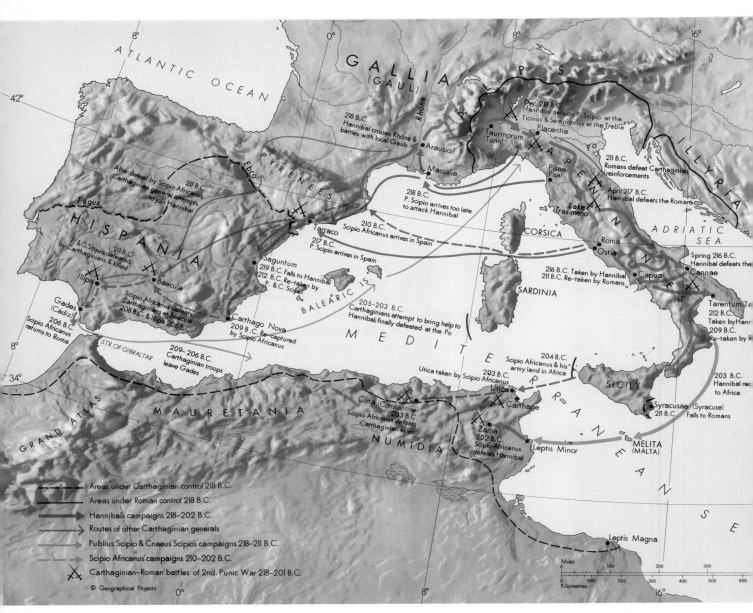

Early in 218 B.C., when Carthage received a war ultimatum from Rome, Hannibal's strong force of infantry and cavalry, backed by 37 elephants, was assembled at Carthago Nova (Cartagena) in southeastern Spain. Hannibal at once decided to march through southern France into Italy. Rome, expecting him to hug the Mediterranean coast, sent an army to intercept him near Massalia (Marseilles). But that army failed in its mission. Hannibal had taken a more northerly inland route through the Alps into the Po valley, and not until December, when he reached it, did he give battle.

Then, at the Battle of Trebia, he used 3,000 of his 6,000 cavalry to outflank the army of Sempronius, attack it from the rear and put it to flight. Four months later he won a second great battle at Lake Trasimeno, 100 miles (160 kilometres) north of Rome; and in 216 B.C. he was again victorious at Cannae, in southeast Italy. Thereafter his fortunes flagged, partly because he lacked the siege equipment—and the military strength—to take Rome and other walled Italian cities, and partly because Carthage failed to send him reinforcements.

Scipio Africanus

The long period of stalemate that followed was finally broken by a brilliant young Roman commander, Publius Cornelius Scipio, soon to gain fame as Scipio Africanus. Scipio insisted on carrying the war to the enemy's camp. From 210 to 206 B.C. he

Below: Two stages in the Battle of Zama. Scipio began by drawing up his cohorts one behind another, with open lanes between them. When Hannibal's elephants charged, some were driven back, terrified by noise from the Roman ranks, while others passed through the open lanes. The Roman cavalry wings then attacked the inferior Carthaginian cavalry wings and routed them. Next (stage 2), the Roman infantry closed up and clashed with the well-matched infantry of Carthage. But soon the Roman cavalry returned from pursuing the Carthaginian cavalry, and attacked Hannibal's infantry from the rear. From that moment the Carthaginians' position was utterly hopeless.

☐	Roman cavalry
▨	Roman infantry
☐	Carthaginian cavalry
■	Carthaginian infantry
🐘	Elephants

fought the Carthaginians in their Spanish provinces, first capturing their great stronghold of Carthago Nova and eventually driving them out of the country. Then in 204 B.C. he sailed from Sicily with two legions to attack North Africa, the Carthaginians' homeland.

He first laid siege to Utica, only a few miles from Carthage itself. But, threatened by a far stronger Carthaginian force, he had to abandon the operation. Carthage offered peace talks and Scipio agreed. Then, while negotiations were proceeding, he fired and attacked the Carthaginian camps by night, destroying shelters, slaying some 40,000 men and capturing many prisoners and horses. He was then able to defeat the depleted Carthaginian army in battle.

Scipio had now achieved his main aim. Carthage, in alarm, recalled Hannibal's army from Italy; and Hannibal, unable to ship his horses home, slew them before embarking. So when he faced Scipio at the Battle of Zama, south of Carthage, in 202 B.C., he had only a hastily raised cavalry arm.

Hannibal drew up his infantry—well matched with Scipio's—in three lines, one behind the other, with cavalry on either side. In front of all he placed what he had but Scipio had not—a line of 80 elephants. Instead of drawing up the Roman cohorts in the usual checker-board fashion, Scipio deployed them one behind the other, three deep, with open lanes from front to back between them. In the lanes—which he hoped the elephants would pass through—he placed his *velites*, to attack the elephants with throwing-spears. On either side he had strong cavalry wings to face Hannibal's weaker counterparts.

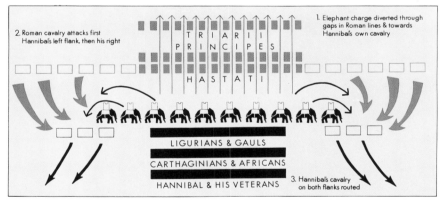

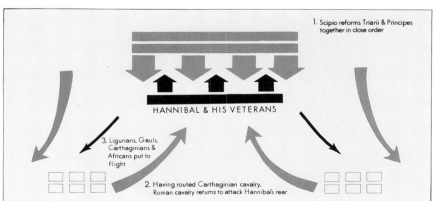

Hannibal

Immediately battle was joined, Hannibal's elephants charged. The Romans sounded trumpets and horns, and about half the elephants rushed back, terrified, into Hannibal's two cavalry wings, which Rome's superior cavalry was then easily able to put to flight. The rest of the elephants charged down the Roman army's open lanes, inflicting severe damage on the *velites*. Meanwhile Scipio's remaining cavalry attacked, routed and pursued Hannibal's right cavalry wing.

This left the field to the evenly matched infantry forces. For a time the battle hung in the balance; then the Romans slowly began driving the Carthaginians back. At this point the Roman cavalry returned from pursuing the enemy horsemen, attacked Hannibal's infantry from the rear and completed Scipio's triumph.

By winning the Second Punic War, Rome gained a foothold in North Africa and won control of Spain and most of the west Mediterranean islands. Thereafter she went on to build up the mightiest empire of the ancient world.

Right until the fourth and early fifth centuries A.D., Rome's legions, reorganized from time to time and eventually recruited as much from barbarian as from Roman sources, constituted the main bulwark of western civilization against the increasing pressure of nomads sweeping westwards from east-central Asia and southwards from Scandinavia. Only in China, where the Great Wall, with a length of 1,400 miles (2,240 kilometres), was completed for the country's defence at the very time of the Second Punic War, did any bulwark hold out longer against the incessant onslaughts of nomadic hordes.

Above: Detail from a Roman column, showing infantry in "testudo" (tortoise) formation. When Roman infantrymen came under very heavy missile fire while besieging a town, soldiers in the front rank lifted their shields up before them, while those in all the other ranks raised their shields above their heads. The whole formation was thus sheathed like a giant tortoise.

Right: Winter along the Great Wall of China. Numerous stretches of wall were built in northern China during the fourth and third centuries B.C., as bulwarks against nomadic hordes. During the reign of the Ch'in Emperor Shi Huang Ti, while the Second Punic War was raging in the West, all these stretches were joined, strengthened and extended, to form a continuous defence work covering a distance equal to that from Rome to Moscow.

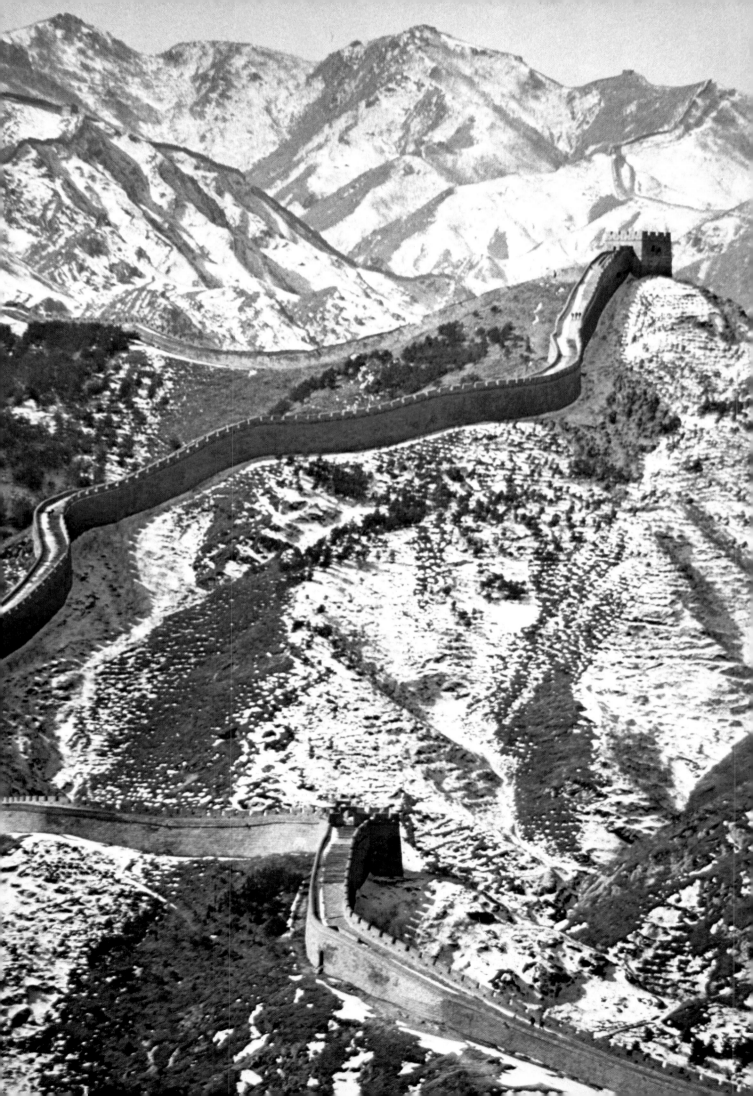

3 Cavalry Warfare

From the time of Alexander the Great to the beginning of the nomad invasions, cavalry had played a steadily growing part in warfare. During much of the next 1,000 years the mounted warrior, far more mobile than infantry and even chariotry, all but ousted the foot soldier from the world's battlefields.

Mainly responsible for this transformation were the nomadic Goths, Huns and Vandals who poured into Europe from north and east during the fourth and fifth centuries A.D. All were men whose way of life had long accustomed them to living in the saddle, an invention that had reached them from the Far East; and the Goths, a Teutonic people originating in Sweden, also brought with them an epoch-making innovation in horsemanship—the stirrup. With stirrups the Gothic heavy cavalryman could keep a far firmer seat in the saddle, while attacking or being attacked, than his stirrupless enemy. He could therefore wield his weapons more effectively.

The Goths, under their leader Fridigern, first demonstrated the ascendancy of heavy cavalry over infantry in A.D. 378, when they soundly defeated a Roman army led by Emperor Valens. The battle was fought near Adrianople, in Thrace.

Eight miles from the city the Goths had set up their *laager*. This was a huge circle of wagons, inside which their women and children were protected by foot soldiers, leaving the more numerous cavalry free to sally out on raids or foraging expeditions. When the Roman army reached the laager, after marching from Adrianople in gruelling heat, Valens artfully agreed to Fridigern's request for peace talks. This would give Valens time to rest his troops and deploy them—strong infantry lines in the centre, flanked on either side by cavalry wings. Fridigern was also merely playing for time, because the bulk of his colossal cavalry force was out foraging.

Before the sham peace parley had properly started, Fridigern had gained all the time he needed. While the Roman cavalry

An early encounter between Goths and Romans. The Romans are almost all foot soldiers, and the few who are mounted lack stirrups—a Gothic innovation that gave the rider a firmer seat in the saddle and allowed him to wield his weapons more effectively.

was edging near the laager and the infantry was still forming up, the Gothic cavalry returned in overwhelming force and quickly routed first the Roman right cavalry wing, then the left. Valens' infantry was then left alone to withstand a combined cavalry and infantry attack. The outcome was scarcely in doubt. By nightfall some 40,000 men—the greater part of the Roman force—had been killed, among them the emperor himself. This disaster marked a major step towards the military collapse of Rome.

After the Goths came an even more formidable horse-borne horde—the Huns. Riding out from north of the Caspian Sea in the mid-fourth century A.D., they had swept beyond the Black

Above: Map showing invasions and war-like migrations in Europe, North Africa and western Asia from the second to the ninth centuries A.D. The coming of the horse-borne Goths, Huns and Vandals ushered in the long age of cavalry warfare. The Moslem invaders of Spain and southern France were also fine horsemen, but the Franks who faced them at Tours in 732 fought and won on foot.

Right: Mediaeval manuscript illumination showing the use of "Greek fire." This oily substance, which contained quicklime and burst into flame as soon as it touched water, was first used against Arab ships around A.D. 700.

34

Sea by A.D. 372. Some 70 years later, led by Attila, they surged westwards beyond the Rhine, in an orgy of plunder and destruction. Their horsemanship was legendary, and it was said that their tough steppe-bred mounts could cover 100 miles (160 kilometres) in a day. Experts with the bow—which they made from horn and spliced wood—and wielding iron swords, they long seemed invincible. Their victorious progress was, however, halted at Châlons in Gaul in A.D. 451, when they were defeated by a combined force, mainly of Romans and Visigoths (West Goths), led by Aëtius. This strange alliance of Romans and Goths shows how serious the Hun menace had become!

The Battle of Châlons ranks as the first almost all-cavalry battle. Infantry, which the Romans themselves had now virtually discarded in favour of mounted troops, played no effective part in it. It was wheeling and charging horsemen armed with bow and lance who dominated the field and decided the day; and it was the heavy Gothic cavalry that overcame the more lightly armed Huns. This defeat was almost the end for the Hun invaders. With Attila's death two years later they ceased to be a menace.

Châlons was Imperial Rome's last major victory in the West. Indeed, within half a century the Ostrogoths (East Goths) were in control of most of Italy. After that, the great military tradition of Rome was carried on by the Eastern Roman Empire, otherwise called the Byzantine Empire, from its capital Byzantium (Constantinople). Byzantium's most famous general was Belisarius. In the 20 years from A.D. 533 onwards, Belisarius reconquered the North African empire that the Vandals, another powerful and far-conquering nomad horde, had snatched from Rome; and with the support of a colleague, Narses, he drove the Ostrogoths from Italy.

These resounding victories were won almost entirely with cavalry. The heavy cavalry, clad in mail and carrying a small shield, wielded lance and either broadsword or axe. The light cavalry, less heavily protected, fought with the bow, although some cavalrymen also carried feathered darts for close-quarter fighting. And backing this highly trained cavalry force was a motley infantry army of mercenaries.

Belisarius himself was an exponent of dash and boldness. These were the qualities that, in 534, ensured his decisive victory over the Vandals at Tricameron, just west of Carthage. Without waiting for his lagging infantry to catch up, he led his 5,000-strong cavalry force across a shallow stream to attack the numerically superior but unready enemy cavalry on the opposite bank and resoundingly defeated it. Later, in Italy, after his small force had entered Rome without a fight, by courtesy of the Pope (who disobeyed the Ostrogothic king), he withstood a year's siege, during which his cavalry frequently sallied from the city and outfought the Ostrogothic horsemen.

Belisarius strengthened the Eastern Empire by building up an army capable of reversing the nomad invaders' long run of success. And by continuing attention to military matters the empire endured a further 900 years, despite constant attacks by

Mediaeval illustration of Carolingian cavalrymen. Charlemagne's decision to rely less on infantry, more on well-armed and well-armoured cavalry, was not easy to implement, because of the high cost of armour, armourers, grooms and strong horses. The difficulty was overcome by making grants of land in return for military service, thus encouraging the growth of feudalism.

Bulgars, Slavs, Persians, Arab Moslems, Christian Crusaders, Turkish Moslems and a host of others.

Cavalry changed little, except that mounted men were in time issued with steel helmets. Heavy and light infantry—the former mail-clad and bearing shield, lance and sword or axe, the latter serving as both bowmen and axemen—improved somewhat. Artillery equipped with catapults, missile-hurling *ballistas* and *trebuchets* (huge counter-weighted slings) played a growing part in siege warfare. Back-up troops included ambulancemen and corps of engineers.

Yet Byzantium's comparatively small standing army would not have been equal, of itself, to her defence needs. The deficiency was made good by massive defence works along the frontiers and by the strong fortress of Byzantium (Constantinople) itself.

In addition Byzantium had one master weapon that her enemies lacked—Greek fire. This highly inflammable oily substance—discharged from some sort of machine—ignited immediately on contact with water, and on more than one occasion it wrought havoc among enemy ships.

Before and during the victories of Belisarius a new power was arising in far-off northwest Europe. The Franks, a warlike Germanic people, were pushing out from their homeland to found a kingdom that, by the start of the seventh century A.D., covered nearly all France, half of Germany and what are now the Low Countries and Switzerland.

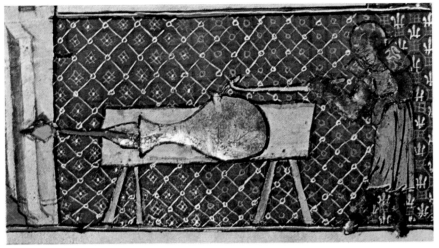

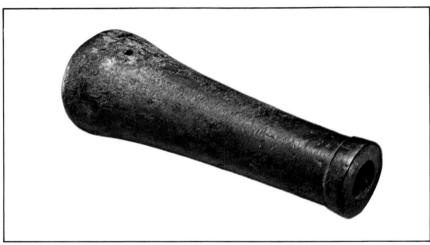

was soon to change the balance of power in western Europe no less than the cannon had changed it in the Balkans.

Towards the close of the fifteenth century, Spain, formerly a divided country, had been unified by the marriage of King Ferdinand of Aragon to Queen Isabella of Castile. Then in 1492—the year of Columbus's first great voyage—the Spaniards had expelled the last of the Moslem Moors from their land. Ferdinand, revelling in Spain's new-found strength, at once became ambitious to extend his influence in Italy, where France also had powerful interests. As a result the two countries were soon at war. And it was in that war, at the Battle of Cerignola in 1503, that the famous Spanish commander Gonzalo de Córdoba put the arquebus to its first real test.

He armed some of his infantry with the new weapon and entrenched them on a slope, along with—but ahead of—his pikemen. The French pikemen and men-at-arms, lured forward by Córdoba's light cavalry, charged against the thin line of Spanish arquebusiers—to be mown down at close quarters by a withering hail of shot that killed their commander, General Nemours. The Spanish arquebusiers and pikemen then emerged from their trenches to complete the victory.

Cerignola marked the beginnings of Spain's rise to military prominence, and other victories soon followed, notably that at

Top left: This picture, which appeared in a manuscript of 1326, is the first known illustration of a gun. It tries to capture the bolt emerging from the barrel, at the very instant of firing.
Left: Bronze gun from southern Sweden, probably cast before 1400. It may well be the oldest gun yet found.
Above: Contemporary illustration of cannon and mortar at one of the sieges of Pampeluna. Stone-shot ammunition can be seen in the foreground.

Right: The "Dardanelles Gun," now to be seen at the Tower of London. Cast in bronze and weighing nearly 19 tons, it is 17 feet (5.18 metres) long, has a calibre of 25 inches (63.5 centimetres), and was capable of firing a shot weighing 800 pounds (362 kilograms). The Dardanelles Gun was cast in 1464, and is very similar to those used at the siege of Constantinople.

46

Pavia in 1525, when the French king was captured and forced to sign a treaty renouncing all his claims in Italy. And because King Charles of Spain, who succeeded Ferdinand, was a Hapsburg and also Holy Roman Emperor, Spain played a major part in most of the conflicts that ravaged western Europe throughout the sixteenth century. What is more, despite all her European commitments, Spain meanwhile found enough men, horses and guns to conquer and consolidate a vast overseas empire in the horseless, gunless New World.

Throughout the fifteenth and sixteenth centuries gunpowder and guns were steadily changing the whole face of warfare. First, their destructive power made fighting more ruthless and put an end to the age of chivalry. Next, gunfire made the old-style mediaeval strongholds as ineffective as the heavily armoured knights who had once defended them. And for a time at least, the importance of cavalry declined sharply, simply because it was impossible for a mounted man to handle and fire the awkward hand guns of the period.

Above all, gunpowder weapons multiplied far faster than the weapons of earlier times. The fifteenth century witnessed the appearance of smoke balls, fire balls, explosive bombs, explosive bronze shells, incendiary shells and the first primitive pistols. During the sixteenth century came improved hand grenades, a crude forerunner of the shrapnel shell, paper cartridges, fixed cartridges (powder and ball in one), rifle-barrelled pistols and— perhaps most important of all—the wheel-lock. This was a device rather like the flint and wheel of a cigarette lighter, for igniting the charge in a musket or pistol. Because wheel-lock pistols could

be fired with one hand only, they became the first firearms that could be used by a man on horseback.

All these innovations followed in such quick succession that no single army could afford to adopt all of them the moment they became available. So for many years armies commonly employed a hotchpotch of weapons, some ancient, some modern, some their own, some captured from enemies.

Europe's almost constant religious and dynastic wars throughout the age of early gun warfare gave commanders ample opportunity to experiment with new tactics and new methods of organization, to make the best use of the ever-changing weapons.

At first the arquebusier had been a mere ancillary to the massed phalanx of pikemen. But as the number of arquebusiers increased, they and the pikemen became arms of equal importance, each designed and drilled to support the other. Then, gradually, the arquebus was ousted by the early musket, a weapon that could fire a far heavier missile but required 56 drill movements to reload. In the Dutch War of Independence (1568–1609), Maurice of Nassau, fighting against Spain, employed musketeers and pikemen in units of men ten ranks deep, with the musketeers on the flanks. When the leading musketeers had fired, they withdrew to the rear of the ranks to reload.

Cavalrymen, whose importance had declined at the start of the sixteenth century, began to come into their own again with the advent of the wheel-lock pistol. They were used in an attacking column that employed a tactic known as the *caracole*. After each rank of the advancing column had fired, it wheeled off so that the following rank could fire.

In the fifteenth century, castles had proved so ineffective against artillery that most decisive battles had to be fought in the open. But by about 1525, castles were rapidly giving way to new-style fortifications, in which high walls were replaced by low ones, protected by a rampart, a ditch, a sloping bank called a *glacis* and earthworks that could absorb the impact of heavy missiles. Further, these forts could hit back hard against attackers, for they were equipped with strongly gunned four-sided turrets that offered defenders a clear view of the enemy and provided for maximum cross fire. And because they were no easy obstacles to overrun, open fighting tended to give place to siege warfare.

Although the nations of sixteenth-century Europe maintained only small armies of around 40,000 men and relied heavily on mercenaries, the end of the century saw the beginnings of the modern command structure and rank system. The company, with its sergeants and corporals, was commanded by a captain commissioned by the sovereign, and a group of companies was in the charge of a lieutenant-colonel. The whole army was commanded by a lieutenant-general, representing the sovereign. But the national army in the full sense had not yet emerged. The

Europe in 1519. By that time gun warfare had already begun to change the destinies of nations. In 1453 the Ottoman Turks had employed immensely heavy guns to bring about the fall of Constantinople. Now they were masters of the greater part of the Balkan Peninsula. In 1503 the Spaniards had defeated the French at Cerignola with the help of hand guns. Now Spain was the leading power in Europe. Crossed-sword symbols mark the sites of other gun-dominated battles of the next 250 years.

48

ARCTIC CIRCLE 66°

8°   0°   8°   16°   24°   32°   40°   48°   56°

FEROE IS.
Denmark

SHETLAND IS.
Scotland

ORKNEY IS.
Scotland

SCOTLAND

NORTH

SEA

D E N M A R K

Oslo •

Norway

S W E D E N

Stockholm •

Finland

Lake
Onega

Lake
Ladoga

R U S S I A

Moscow •

Northern Dvina

Volga

Volga

BALTIC SEA

TEUTONIC
ORDER

Riga •

Smolensk •

Don

Dnieper

L I T H U A N I A

TEUTONIC
ORDER

Prussia

Copenhagen •

• Hamburg

H O L Y

LUSATIA

• Cologne

Breitenfeld ✕

Elbe

R O M A N

BOHEMIA

SILESIA

MORAVIA

Odra

Vistula

Warsaw •

P O L A N D

Dnieper

Dnieper

KHANATE

OF CRIMEA

Crimea

ENGLAND

Oudenarde ✕✕
Brussels ✕ Ramillies ✕
Malplaquet ✕

Paris •

FRANCE

BOURBON
LANDS

Fr. crown
1527

Rhine

Blenheim ✕
Bavaria •

E M P I R E

Danube

Vienna •

Austria

Buda •

H U N G A R Y

Hungary, Bohemia, Lusatia, Silesia &
Moravia united under same crown from 1490

BURGUNDY

SWISS
CONFEDERATIONS

Bern •

Rhône

D. OF
SAVOY
Turin •

D. OF
MILAN
Pavia
MILAN ✕

Po

Venice •

REP. OF VENICE

Danube

BLACK SEA

Papal
States

Genoa •

REP. OF
GENOA
Fr. 1499-1512,
1515-28

REP. OF
FLORENCE
• Florence

Siena

PAPAL
STATES

MONTE-
NEGRO

O T T O M A N

Constantinople •

DUCHY OF MILAN
Fr. 1499-1512, 1515-21

CORSICA
Genoa

REP. OF
SIENA

Rome •

Benevento ✕✕
Cerignola ✕

NAPLES
Sp. 1504

K. OF
Naples •

42°

IS.

SARDINIA
Spain

E

D

I

T

E

R

R

A

N

E

A

N

S E A

Bougie
Sp. 1510-55

Bône
Sp. 1535-74

Bizerte
Sp. 1535-74

Palermo •

SICILY
Spain 1504

• MALTA
Sp.
Knights of St. John 1530

OTTOMAN
EMPIRE

Tunisia

CRETE

Venice •

KHIOS
Genoa

RHODES
Knights of St. John
Ottoman Empire 1522

CYPRUS
Ottoman Empire 1507

E M P I R E

Miles
0   100   200   300   400   500

0 100 200 300 400 500 600 700 800
Kilometres

48°

58°

50°

40°

42°

34°

8°   16°   24°   32°

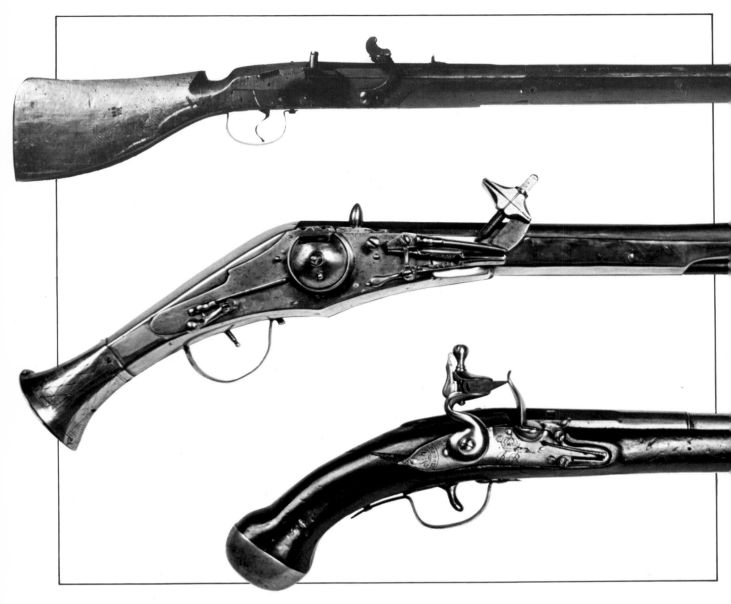

troops could not rely on regular pay; they had to bear part of the cost of their equipment and rations; and provisioning was in the sometimes dubious hands of private contractors.

In the constant continental warfare of the time, England played little part. Occupied mainly with her own internal affairs, she maintained no national army and felt no need to adopt new land-fighting techniques. Her traditional weapons were still the halberd-like bill and the longbow, and not until the reign of Elizabeth I (1558–1603) did England replace the longbow with the arquebus. The nation's main energies went into the development of her sea power, in which she became the chief rival of Europe's most powerful sea-going nation, Spain. During the reign of Henry VIII (1509–47) she developed the first sailing ship capable of delivering a broadside; and by the time of Elizabeth I, England's navy was powerful enough first to harass Spanish shipping in the Caribbean and finally to defeat the mighty Spanish Armada that attempted to invade England in 1588.

Three types of hand gun, together with diagrams of their firing mechanisms: matchlock (top), wheel-lock (centre) and flint-lock (bottom). The first hand guns had no automatic firing mechanism. The gunner had to set a glowing slow match to the powder in the pan while taking aim. The first mechanism, used in the arquebus, was the matchlock. In essence it was a curved, pivoted lever, the top of which was fitted with a clip to hold the glowing match. When the gunner pulled the trigger, the lever moved, bringing the match against the pan. The wheel-lock, which followed, needed no slow match. Its essential parts were a steel disc with a serrated edge and a fixed piece of iron pyrites. A squeeze of the trigger set the disc spinning; its edge rubbed against the pyrites and produced sparks that fell onto the powder. Later, in the flint-lock, the trigger movement produced two simultaneous effects. It lifted the pan cover and brought flint against steel to strike the necessary sparks.

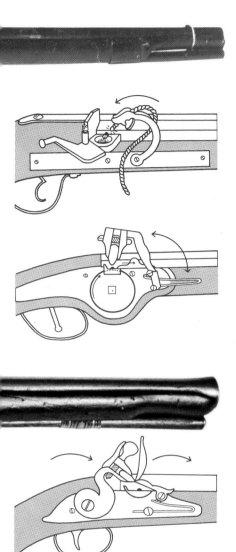

While England was still concentrating on naval affairs, land warfare in Europe was beginning to assume a more modern aspect. In the early seventeenth century armies grew larger and tended to become permanent; the scale of fighting expanded; and the cost and complexity of war making steadily increased.

These tendencies manifested themselves sharply during the Thirty Years' War (1618–48). For several years of that savage and devastating conflict, in which alliances and even objectives frequently changed, the main contestants were on one side the Catholic Holy Roman Emperor Ferdinand II, backed by Catholic Spain and Bavaria, and on the opposing side Catholic France, in alliance with the Protestant German states and Protestant Sweden. And in the struggle, King Gustavus Adolphus of Sweden emerged as the father of modern warfare.

Besides building the first professional army for foreign service, Gustavus Adolphus also introduced a wide range of innovations and reforms that made the Swedish army the best in Europe—a well-trained, versatile fighting machine backed by highly efficient engineering, technical and medical services. He replaced the musketeer's heavy wooden rest with a light iron spike, thus increasing the musketeer's mobility; later the king issued lighter muskets that required no rest; and by arming the musketeer with a sword, he gave him an added means of defence. The king also introduced the paper cartridge, which reduced the number of reloading movements, thus allowing a greater rate of fire. This led to a significant change in battle drill. The old ten-rank formation was replaced by a T-shaped three-rank grouping, in which all three ranks fired simultaneously, the front rank, forming the stem of the T, kneeling while the others stood. So devastating were these volleys that the number of pikemen needed for hand-to-hand fighting was drastically reduced, and in time the old massed array of pikes vanished altogether.

But in his long career Gustavus Adolphus did much besides improving musketry. Departing from the custom of deploying

Mounted men armed with wheel-lock weapons attack infantry armed with matchlocks, in a German battle fought in 1636. Before the advent of the wheel-lock it was almost impossible for cavalrymen to use hand guns.

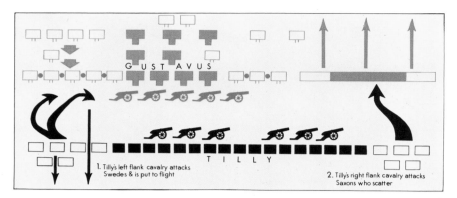

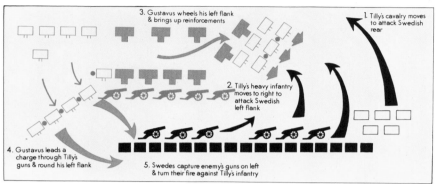

© Geographical Projects

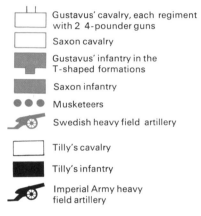

Gustavus' cavalry, each regiment with 2 4-pounder guns

Saxon cavalry

Gustavus' infantry in the T-shaped formations

Saxon infantry

Musketeers

Swedish heavy field artillery

Tilly's cavalry

Tilly's infantry

Imperial Army heavy field artillery

units of up to 3,000 troops for battle, he split his forces into units of 500 or less, thus ensuring higher flexibility and lower vulnerability to artillery fire. He also restored the shock-troop role of cavalry, training them to rely mainly on the sword, although they also used the pistol for close work; and he instituted the first dragoons—troops acting as light cavalry in attack and as infantry in defence. Besides increasing the quota of artillery in his army, he standardized it into three main types—siege, field and regimental. Further, he reduced the weight of field and regimental guns, thus producing a light, mobile artillery that could easily be integrated with infantry regiments. In addition, he introduced the first artillery cartridge, a novelty that increased safety in handling and significantly stepped up the rate of fire. Above all, he raised morale by such measures as issuing pay regularly, standardizing and improving the quality of uniforms, instituting military badges and attaching chaplains to the force.

Of all the battles the Swedish army won during the Thirty Years' War, perhaps the most memorable was that fought at Breitenfeld, near Leipzig, in 1631. There the forces of the Holy Roman Empire, led by Count Tilly, were an equal match numerically for the 40,000-strong Swedish army. Gustavus Adolphus won a brilliant victory, owing mainly to the greater mobility of his musketeers and pikemen, and their close coordination with his cavalry and artillery.

Before the Thirty Years' War ended, England was again giving attention to military matters. In the Civil War between king and Parliament (1642–45) the Parliamentary forces were reorganized at the instance of the Puritan leader, Oliver Cromwell, to form the New Model Army under General Fairfax. Well

Right: Model of Sebastien de Vauban's fortress at Neuf Brisach, one of several massive defences that he constructed in the vulnerable gap between the Jura and the Vosges, on France's eastern frontier. Vauban fortresses bristled with strong angular projections from which an attack from any direction could be brought under lethal fire. The only hope of taking such a fortress was by laying siege to it. And it was Vauban himself who worked out the elaborate siege tactics that would be needed to achieve success.

trained, well disciplined and capably officered, this was the first regular British army. It comprised 11 cavalry and 12 infantry regiments—the latter with a musketeer-to-pikeman ratio of two to one—and an artillery arm with four types of field gun. The musketeers were armed with an improved lighter musket, the matchlock being replaced with the wheel-lock and flint-lock. The New Model Army proved itself in 1645, when it decisively defeated the Royalist forces at Naseby.

Europe's later seventeenth-century wars—mainly the campaigns of the ambitious French ruler Louis XIV—produced an outstanding military engineer, Sebastien de Vauban (1633–1707). Vauban, who fortified France's vulnerable frontiers with a series of powerful fortresses and citadels, was a master of both defensive fortification and offensive siege craft. He based his ingenious fortification system on geometric principles, strengthening the central defences with large bastions at the main angular points of the walls, and with smaller bastions, able to give mutual cover, along the walls themselves. He also extended his outworks well away from the inner fortress, thus forcing the attacker to overcome a network of preliminary obstacles almost impossible to surmount by direct attack.

In the matter of offence, Vauban evolved a system of "parallels and approaches," by which the besiegers advanced from one parallel trench to the next by way of shorter connecting zigzag trenches. Vauban's defensive and siege techniques persisted unchanged for many years, greatly hampering mobility.

But there was still room on Europe's battlefields for brilliant aggressive generalship, and in John Churchill (later Duke of Marlborough), England produced the greatest soldier of the

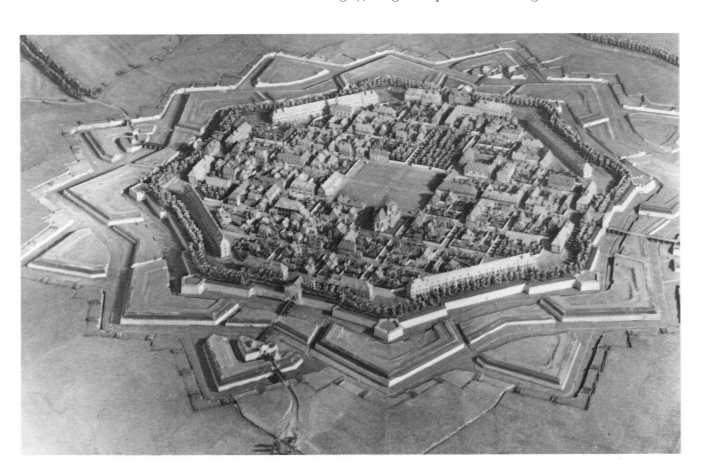

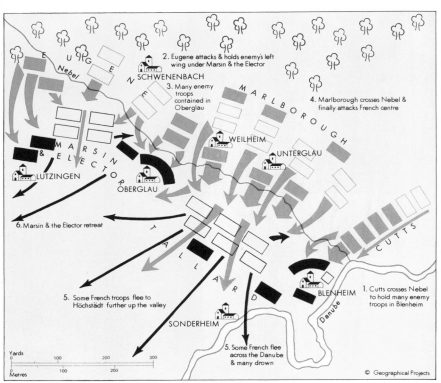

2. Eugene attacks & holds enemy's left wing under Marsin & the Elector

SCHWENENBACH

3. Many enemy troops contained in Oberglau

MARLBOROUGH

4. Marlborough crosses Nebel & finally attacks French centre

Nebel

WEILHEIM

UNTERGLAU

MARSIN & ELECTOR

LÜTZINGEN

OBERGLAU

6. Marsin & the Elector retreat

TALLARD

CUTTS

5. Some French troops flee to Höchstädt further up the valley

BLENHEIM

Danube

1. Cutts crosses Nebel to hold many enemy troops in Blenheim

SONDERHEIM

5. Some French flee across the Danube & many drown

Yards
0   100   200   300
Metres
0   100   200

© Geographical Projects

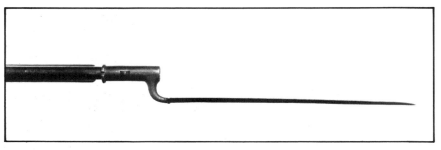

era. Commanding the British and Dutch armies (as part of an alliance that also included the armies of Austria and most of the German states) against France, Spain and Bavaria in the War of the Spanish Succession (1701–14), Marlborough won a series of famous victories at Blenheim (1704), Ramillies (1706), Oudenarde (1708) and Malplaquet (1709).

The British musketeer of this period benefited from an important innovation, the ring-bayonet, which remained fixed to the barrel of his musket even during firing, thus allowing him to combine the roles of musketeer and pikeman, so that pikemen as such were no longer required. Marlborough, in his determination to bring out the maximum effectiveness of all arms, insisted on accuracy in musketry fire, with simultaneous firing by all ranks; he stressed the importance of momentum, rather than firing, in the cavalry charge; and he placed great weight on the offensive impact of artillery—an arm he handled with notable skill.

The Battle of Blenheim—a Bavarian village on the Danube—was a notable example of Marlborough's generalship. The French and Bavarians held a strongly fortified position behind the Nebel, a stream flowing into the Danube, with their right flank resting on that river. Facing them across the Nebel was Marlborough's army of 56,000 men, slightly outnumbered by the enemy.

Above: A splendid tapestry commemorating the Battle of Blenheim, won by the combined armies of Britain, under the Duke of Marlborough, and of Austria, under Prince Eugene of Savoy.

Above left: Plan showing the main events of the battle. By crossing the Nebel, the force under Cutts' command pinned down a large number of enemy troops in Blenheim, while Eugene attacked and held the enemy left wing, containing a further large number of the enemy in Oberglau. All this meant that the French centre was badly weakened when Marlborough crossed the Nebel to attack it. So successful was the attack that the French troops were forced to flee whichever way they could—some going southwest to Höchstädt, others south across the Danube (where many met their deaths by drowning), and yet others to the west.

☐ Marlborough's cavalry

▨ Marlborough's infantry

☐ French cavalry

■ French infantry

Commanding on his left flank was Lord Cutts, and on his right his ally Prince Eugene of Savoy, while Marlborough himself was in the centre. Cutts opened with an attack on Blenheim, but was twice repulsed with heavy losses. Then, while Cutts kept up a feint assault on Blenheim (drawing many troops to its defence) and Prince Eugene attacked on the right towards the village of Oberglau (involving yet more of the enemy), Marlborough—having achieved his aim to stretch and weaken his opponent's centre—led his troops across the Nebel, breached the thinly manned enemy ranks and enveloped the French right, driving thousands of them into the Danube. His victory was complete.

On a par with Marlborough as an outstanding commander was Frederick II of Prussia—Frederick the Great. Inheriting a fine and greatly expanded army from his father—Frederick William I, whom he succeeded in 1740—Frederick improved and toughened it by rigid discipline, meticulous drilling and exhaustive training in battle movements and weapon handling to make it the most efficient fighting force in Europe. Essentially an attacking general, Frederick based both his strategy and his tactics on mobility and aggressiveness. These qualities were apparent in all his campaigns, which started a year after his accession, when he made war on Austria and invaded Silesia. His army was generally outnumbered by its adversaries, but this disadvantage was compensated for by his infantry's greater rate of fire—the result of constantly rehearsed reloading drill. But more important still was his use of horse artillery, an arm that owed its origin to the fact that field guns were now light enough to be drawn swiftly by horses instead of slowly by bullocks. And always, behind the Prussian army, was a military state whose strict organization for war foreshadowed future trends.

5 Towards Total Warfare

The closing years of the eighteenth century ushered in a period of massive change in the conduct and motivation of war. Dominated by the wars sparked off by the French Revolution (1789) and the long Napoleonic conflict that followed, warfare emerged from its old restricted character to become an activity that occupied a great part of the resources of many nations. The standing army fighting at the whim of one royal house to unseat another gave place to the huge conscript army, fighting with motives the common soldier understood and shared. In France the motives were to safeguard the Revolution or, under the empire-building leadership of Napoleon Bonaparte, to achieve total conquest. In the nations that opposed France the aims were to stem the tide of revolution, and later to thwart Napoleon's ambitions.

The enlarged scale of warfare was made possible by two sweeping changes—the Industrial Revolution and the Agrarian Revolution. The first provided mass-produced and more accurately engineered munitions, together with newly built canals and better road-maintenance methods, improving military transport. The second vastly augmented food supplies available for the growing populations from which large armies were recruited.

Eighteenth-century France had already developed a number of war making improvements, notably in artillery; standardized—and therefore interchangeable—parts for guns and gun carriages; hardwood axles in place of heavy iron ones; and a new "tangent" sight, which enabled guns to be laid more accurately. Meanwhile, advances in mathematics were everywhere improving the art of producing military maps; and before the century ended, France had introduced a system of long-distance signalling by means of high, windmill-like semaphore posts.

Equally important was the military thinking that went on in France shortly before 1792, when she went to war with Austria and Prussia, the countries that—later joined by Britain, the

French artillery in action during the Napoleonic campaigns. New industrial methods made it possible to produce heavy guns on a large scale, and Napoleon used them lavishly, regarding artillery as the final arbiter in war.

Netherlands and Spain—formed the first coalition against her new revolutionary regime. General Gribeauval had argued the case for greater mobility and offensiveness in warfare; and the military reformer Guibert had advocated the creation of a citizen army, thus foreshadowing the "nation in arms" that materialized with the Revolution.

One result of the French Revolution, with its emphasis on equality, was an increased professionalism in the army. Officers were selected from a much wider class of society than before and given expert training—particularly in gunnery and engineering techniques. (At the turn of the century, military colleges were founded in France, as well as in Britain and the United States.) And when the French victory against the Prussians and Austrians at Valmy on the Aisne (1792) was followed less than a year later by defeats in the Lowlands, there came an immediate and drastic overhaul of France's military system.

Lazare Carnot, a statesman concerned solely with military affairs, employed conscription to raise the strength of the army to half a million men. Because one general alone could not command such a huge force, Carnot split the army not into specialized regiments but into "divisions"—formations comprising all arms, that could operate singly or with other divisions.

Professional efficiency and patriotic fervour, coupled with good discipline and morale, were thus the characteristics of the army soon to be inherited by one of the greatest commanders of all time, Napoleon Bonaparte.

The Corsican-born Bonaparte entered the French army in 1785 as an artillery officer and became a brigadier-general in 1793, at the age of only 24. Three years later he commanded the French army that drove the Austrians out of Italy. In 1798–99 he invaded Egypt, threatening Britain's vital interests in India. In 1802 he became Life Consul of France and in 1804 Emperor. Thereafter, against coalitions that at one time or another comprised most of the nations of Europe, he won battle after historic battle, defeating the Austrians and Russians at Austerlitz in 1805, the Prussians at Jena and Auerstädt in 1806, the Russians again at Friedland in 1807, the Austrians again at Wagram in 1809, the Russians yet again—but this time only narrowly—at Borodino in 1812. Yet there was a debit side to his brilliant record: the disastrous retreat from Moscow in 1812, the crushing defeat of his armies by the allies at the Battle of Leipzig in 1813 and his final defeat by the British and Prussians at Waterloo in 1815.

Strangely, the great campaigns that kept Napoleon's armies fighting across the length and breadth of Europe for nearly 20 years saw few innovations in French weaponry. The infantryman used a muzzle-loading flint-lock musket scarcely changed from the time of Louis XIV; the artilleryman fired guns of virtually pre-Revolutionary pattern; and almost the only improvement in the cavalryman's weapons was a longer lance that could outreach enemy bayonets. Indeed, so indifferent was Napoleon to new devices that in 1799 he disbanded the balloonist corps, the balloon having only recently been introduced as a promising

Spanish guerrillas harassing French troops during the Peninsular campaign. These determined resistance fighters did much to lower French morale, and Napoleon recognized them as major contributors to his ultimate downfall.

observation aid. He also failed to make use of the new shrapnel projectile, invented in the late eighteenth century by the British Colonel Shrapnel. Designed to explode in mid-air and shower bullets down on the enemy, this weapon might have served him well against the famous British "squares" at Waterloo.

Yet outweighing any lack of originality in weapon techniques were Napoleon's outstanding ability as an organizer, his careful planning, his mastery of strategy and tactics and his ability to attract the enthusiastic loyalty of his troops.

Alert to talent wherever it appeared, he created a body of 26 marshals, nearly all of common birth, and built up an efficient staff system under a Chief of Staff. Supplied with a constant stream of information and working with large-scale maps, he then planned the broadest manoeuvres and the most detailed moves alike with a meticulous thoroughness, always taking the final decisions himself.

Although infantry was the chief arm of his armies, and although he attached due importance to the assault power of cavalry, he regarded artillery as the final arbiter in battle.

In an age when siege warfare was going into almost total eclipse, he wisely made offence the hallmark of his strategy and tactics, relying on speed to confuse the enemy with a surprise attack. When the enemy force was numerically weaker than his own, as at the Battle of Ulm (1805), he simply aimed to encircle it and compel a surrender. When it was stronger, he aimed to split it and then attack one part before it could be reinforced. One of his favourite moves was to make a holding attack on the enemy front while some of his divisions wheeled round to attack the enemy rear, threatening their communications. He would then launch a shattering artillery attack on the weakened centre of the line, following it up with a massed cavalry charge.

Military genius, however, was not a French monopoly at this time. In Nelson and Wellington, Britain produced two commanders scarcely less outstanding than Napoleon himself. Between them they played the most vital part of any Allied leaders in defeating the Corsican's far-reaching plans for European conquest.

By his victory at the Battle of the Nile (1798), Nelson cut off Napoleon's Egyptian expedition from its base, so ending the threat to British interests in India; by winning the Battle of Copenhagen (1801) he forced powerful Denmark to withdraw from the French-inspired system of anti-British "armed neutrality"; and at the Battle of Trafalgar (1805) he ended the already weakened possibility of a French invasion of England and ensured British maritime supremacy for the duration of the Napoleonic Wars.

Wellington, who had earlier seen service in India, commanded with distinction in the Peninsular campaign (1804–14), which Britain mounted to encourage Portuguese and Spanish resistance to Napoleon, and to support the local guerrillas—the first irregular fighters to be known by that name—who constantly harassed French troops. But Wellington's biggest

This painting, done on the lid of a snuff box, shows a French observation balloon hovering above the Battle of Fleurus (1794). France was first to recognize the value of balloons for reconnaissance, yet Napoleon was so indifferent to new military devices that he disbanded the balloonist corps when it was only six years old.

challenge came when, with the Prussian army under General Blücher, he faced Napoleon at Waterloo, near Brussels, in 1815.

Early on June 18 the opposing troops—Wellington's British and Dutch force of 67,000 men and 156 guns against the French force of 72,000 men and 246 guns—were drawn up, about a mile apart, on two slopes separated by a valley. At mid-morning the French attacked Wellington's right front at Hougoumont; but this and subsequent assaults, made in strength, were repulsed by the British guardsmen. Some two hours later, after a preliminary artillery bombardment, a French body of 24 battalions, advancing in column, struck at Wellington's left and left centre; but its leading ranks were shattered by British infantry volleys and a follow-up cavalry charge. At 1600 hours the French cavalry furiously attacked Wellington's right centre, charging repeatedly against the hard-pressed British squares, which were also harassed by enemy skirmishers and artillery. At 1830 hours the defenders at La Haye Sainte, in the Allied centre, were forced to surrender through lack of ammunition.

Wellington now faced a crisis. If Napoleon had sent up reinforcements the Allied centre might have been pierced. But he did not, and at that moment relief came. The Prussian force, which had two days earlier suffered a defeat that forced it to withdraw northwards, now entered the picture. Having started to advance at 1630 hours, the Prussians had captured Plancenoit, to the rear of Napoleon's centre, but were later driven out. Then, at 1915 hours, Napoleon ordered his elite French Guard to charge Wellington's right and centre. But by now another Prussian force

Right: Map showing the campaigns in which Napoleon took part in person, from the relief of Toulon in 1793 to the Battle of Waterloo in 1815. During those 22 years his colossal ambition and insatiable appetite for conquest spurred him on to fight in places as far apart as northwest Spain, Moscow and Cairo.

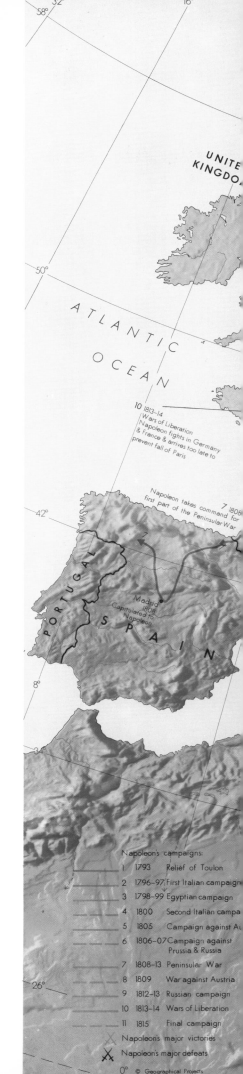

Napoleon's campaigns:

1	1793	Relief of Toulon
2	1796–97	First Italian campaign
3	1798–99	Egyptian campaign
4	1800	Second Italian campaign
5	1805	Campaign against Austria
6	1806–07	Campaign against Prussia & Russia
7	1808–13	Peninsular War
8	1809	War against Austria
9	1812–13	Russian campaign
10	1813–14	Wars of Liberation
11	1815	Final campaign

Napoleon's major victories
Napoleon's major defeats

© Geographical Projects

NORTH
SEA

D E N M A R K

S W E D E N

BALTIC SEA

R U S S I A N

E M P I R E

Volga

9 1812
Start of Napoleon's
Russian campaign

Battle of Borodino
1812
Napoleon defeats Russians

Moscow
1812
Occupied by Napoleon for
5 weeks before he begins
his retreat from Moscow

Königsberg
1807
Occupied

PRUSSIA

Eylau
1807

Friedland
1807

6

Vilnyus
1812
Occupied by
Napoleon

Smolensk
1812
Destroyed by French

1812
Napoleon leaves his
retreating army &
flees to Paris

9

Berlin
1806
Occupied by Napoleon

CONF.

Auerstädt
1806

Leipzig
1813
Napoleon defeated

GRAND-
DUCHY

OF WARSAW

Warsaw

Waterloo
1815

Ligny
1815

nal defeat of Napoleon
by Wellington

OF 10 THE

Jena
1806

10

Laon
1814
on defeated

Paris 10

1806-07
Napoleon's campaign
against Prussia & Russia

Dresden
1813

F R E N C H

Dijon
1800

Start of Napoleon's 2nd.
Italian campaign

5 1805
Start of
campaign against
Austria

RHINE

5

5

8

Austerlitz
1805
Napoleon defeats Austrian & Russian armies

Rhine

Ulm
1805 Taken by French

Wagram
1809 Napoleon defeats Austrians

8 Aspern & Essling
1809 Napoleon defeated for first time

E M P I R E

Rhône

SWITZERLAND

Leoben

2

Vienna
1805
Taken by French
1809
Retaken by French

AUSTRIAN
EMPIRE

Danube

8 1809
Napoleon at war
with Austria

Danube

BLACK SEA

Lodi

11

1

Rhône

4

Marengo
1800

ILLYRIAN
PROVINCES

Toulon
1793
Relief of Toulon

Nice
1796

3

2

Napoleon starts
out on Italian
campaign

KINGDOM
OF ITALY

Ancona

OTTOMAN

MONTE-
NEGRO

3 May 1798
Napoleon sails
from Toulon
for Egypt

11

FRENCH

EMPIRE

ELBA
1815

Napoleon leaves
Elba for his final
campaign

KINGDOM
OF
SARDINIA

KINGDOM
OF NAPLES

FR.

BR.

M E D I T E R

KINGDOM
OF SICILY

BR.

MALTA
(BR.)
June 1798
Taken by Napoleon

R A N E A N   S E A

Battle of the Nile
Aug. 1798
Nelson destroys French fleet

Aug. 1799
Napoleon returns to France

3

Abukir
July 1799
Napoleon defeats
Turks & British

Alexandria
July 1798
Taken by Napoleon

3

MT. TABOR
Apr.

Acre
1799

Napoleon defeats Turks

Jaffa
Mar. 1799
Taken by
Napoleon

O T T O M A N   E M P I R E

Battle of the Pyramids
July 1798

Cairo

3

RED
SEA

Nile

Miles
100   200   300   400   500

Kilometres
100 200 300 400 500 600 700 800

French cavalry attacking British infantry squares at Waterloo. It was immensely difficult for cavalry to break the square formation. The side of the square facing the attack often brought down so many horsemen that the rest were forced to turn and gallop along the adjacent sides, encountering further heavy fire.

A French grenadier of Napoleon's army. He and his comrades were responsible for guarding the Emperor's person and were usually kept in reserve.

had joined the Allied left flank, enabling Wellington to reinforce his threatened front and repulse the French assault. Napoleon had made his last effort. The battle ended with the Prussians pursuing the broken enemy. The French had lost between 30,000 and 40,000 men, including prisoners; the Allied losses were 22,000. For Napoleon the defeat was total and irreversible. Four days later he abdicated.

Just as the British army of the time—not a conscript national force but still a relatively small professional army—differed from the Napoleonic model, so Wellington differed greatly in character from Napoleon. Ruled by a stern sense of duty, he was without personal ambition; and his chief quality as a soldier was steadiness rather than dash. He has been called a cautious and supremely able strategist and a sure and brilliant tactician. Unlike Napoleon, he did not employ massed artillery; but whenever possible he placed his guns on hill tops, where they could rain down shrapnel shells on the enemy. His troops used much the same musket as the French but were trained to face the French columns in linear formation, thus gaining far greater firepower. Further, Wellington employed the ruse of drawing up the bulk of his troops just out of sight of the enemy, over a hill crest. Not only did this shield them from enemy fire; it also confused the enemy, who, when he charged, found himself facing a larger force than he had anticipated.

Yet, like the French, Wellington adopted the divisional formation in place of the regimental structure; and like Napoleon, he made thoroughness his watchword in all things.

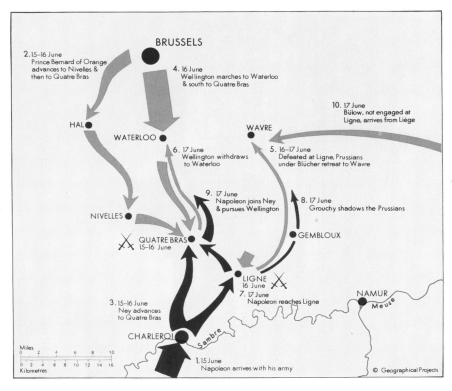

BRUSSELS

2. 15–16 June
Prince Bernard of Orange
advances to Nivelles &
then to Quatre Bras

4. 16 June
Wellington marches to Waterloo
& south to Quatre Bras

10. 17 June
Bülow, not engaged at
Ligne, arrives from Liége

HAL

WATERLOO

WAVRE

6. 17 June
Wellington withdraws
to Waterloo

5. 16–17 June
Defeated at Ligne, Prussians
under Blücher retreat to Wavre

9. 17 June
Napoleon joins Ney
& pursues Wellington

8. 17 June
Grouchy shadows the Prussians

NIVELLES

GEMBLOUX

QUATRE BRAS
15–16 June

LIGNE
16 June

NAMUR

Meuse

7. 17 June
Napoleon reaches Ligne

3. 15–16 June
Ney advances
to Quatre Bras

CHARLEROI

Sambre

Miles
0 2 4 6 8 10
0 2 4 6 8 10 12 14 16
Kilometres

1. 15 June
Napoleon arrives with his army

© Geographical Projects

A British grenadier at the time of
Waterloo. His regiment, which served
with distinction in the battle, was
already a century and a half old.

The brief numbered paragraphs on the plan above show the sequence of events during
the three days preceding the Battle of Waterloo. They explain why the Prussian force,
under the command of Blücher, was at Wavre, some distance to the east of Waterloo,
when the main battle began on June 18. Numbered paragraphs on the plan below show
the sequence of events on that fateful day, from 0600 hours, when Wellington arrived
on the scene, to 1930 hours, when the Prussians came to reinforce his battle-weary
troops and turn the tide of battle in the Allies' favour. Had Napoleon reinforced
his troops at La Haye Sainte an hour earlier, he might well have triumphed.

| | Wellington's cavalry | | Wellington's infantry | | Wellington's tree (his Command Post) |
| | Napoleon's cavalry | | Napoleon's infantry | | |

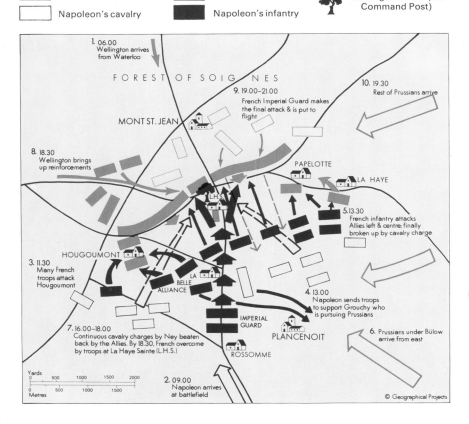

1. 06.00
Wellington arrives
from Waterloo

FOREST OF SOIGNES

9. 19.00–21.00
French Imperial Guard makes
the final attack & is put to
flight

10. 19.30
Rest of Prussians arrive

MONT ST. JEAN

8. 18.30
Wellington brings
up reinforcements

PAPELOTTE

LA HAYE

5. 13.30
French infantry attacks
Allies left & centre; finally
broken up by cavalry charge

L.H.S.

HOUGOUMONT

LA
BELLE
ALLIANCE

3. 11.30
Many French
troops attack
Hougoumont

IMPERIAL
GUARD

4. 13.00
Napoleon sends troops
to support Grouchy who
is pursuing Prussians

PLANCENOIT

6. Prussians under Bülow
arrive from east

7. 16.00–18.00
Continuous cavalry charges by Ney beaten
back by the Allies. By 18.30, French overcome
by troops at La Haye Sainte (L.H.S.)

ROSSOMME

Yards
0 500 1000 1500 2000
0 500 1000 1500
Metres

2. 09.00
Napoleon arrives
at battlefield

© Geographical Projects

After the long-drawn struggle of the Napoleonic Wars, an exhausted Europe settled down to a comparatively long period of peace. The nations were war-weary and financially strained, and needed time for recovery and reconstruction. Very soon armies were drastically cut back: in Britain to a total of 100,000; in France to 150,000. Only two powers, Russia and Prussia, retained their mass wartime armies. In most countries, including military-minded Prussia, the armies tended to revert to their eighteenth-century practice of restricting officership to the privileged classes, and, in Britain in particular, the training of soldiers was virtually confined to the parade ground, with little musket practice.

Four decades of peace and the general slackening of warlike preparedness had their inevitable effects when major hostilities again erupted in Europe in the Crimean War (1854–56). This conflict, in which Britain and France fought to oppose Russian expansion towards the Mediterranean, revealed an appalling state of military incompetence. The British command system, staff work, planning, battle training and tactics, supply and medical organization and co-operation at every level—all showed glaring defects. France's performance was no better.

Nevertheless, the Crimean War had its brighter facets. Several nations, alerted to the dangers of unpreparedness, quickly embarked on a thorough overhaul of their military administration. Florence Nightingale, appalled by reports of the sufferings of the sick and wounded, made the Crimean Peninsula the starting place for a worldwide move towards higher nursing standards and better hospitals. And the new transport methods and new weapons employed in the war took full advantage of the technical possibilities opened up by the ever-increasing use of steam power and the ever-growing scale and precision of industry.

The Prussians and Russians had utilized steam railways for troop movements in the late 1840s. Now, in 1854, British troops sailed to the Crimea in steamships. In the early 1830s, improved mass-engineering techniques had made it possible to furnish the inside of a musket barrel with spiral grooves (rifling), which imparted a rotary motion to the bullet and greatly increased the weapon's range; and by 1840 the British infantryman was discarding the Brown Bess musket, in use since 1640, and taking to the rifle. At first it was a muzzle-loader employing an expanding cartridge case; but by 1853 it employed a percussion firing mechanism of the kind that Prussian rifles had first utilized five years earlier.

In the early 1850s, first breech-loading, then rifling was applied to artillery pieces; and during the Crimean War, breech-loading rifled cannon, with their greater range and accuracy, proved highly effective in the bombardment of the strongly fortified Russian port of Sevastopol.

In 1859, five years after the Crimean War ended, the French, who were supporting the small north Italian state of Piedmont in its war against Austria, used similar guns on a massive scale at the Battle of Solferino. So horrifying was the carnage at that battle that it impelled a Swiss observer, Henri Dunant, to write a

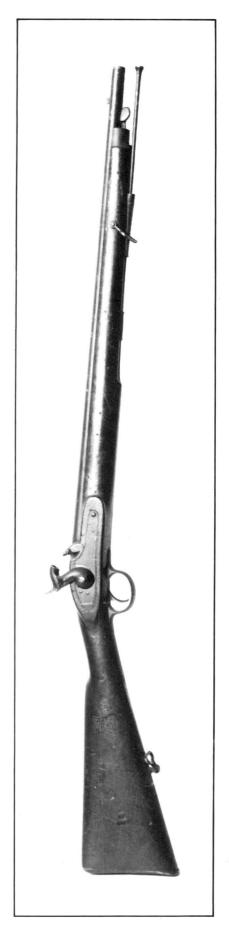

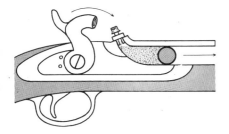

Left: The Enfield percussion rifle of 1853 and (above) its firing mechanism. A small percussion cap was placed over a nipple drilled out to connect with the chamber holding the charge. When the trigger was squeezed the hollowed-out cock struck the cap and set it off, at the same time fitting snugly over it, so that the resulting flash was guided onto the charge. This greatly reduced the risk of misfires.

Below: Scene after the fall of Sevastopol in 1855. Here, at the Redan (a fort), most of the Russian guns had been borrowed from ships of the Black Sea fleet. The defence works had been hurriedly strengthened with gabions—wicker-work cylinders filled with earth—and sandbags.

book, *Un Souvenir de Solferino*, that aroused the world's conscience and was largely instrumental in bringing the International Red Cross organization into being.

Europe's next two wars—the Austro-Prussian War of 1866 and the Franco-Prussian War of 1870–71—were brief; and they were followed by the longest period of peace in the continent's history. Nevertheless, they prepared the ground for future warfare on a more widespread and destructive scale than ever before; for out of them, as a result of the grandiose political ambitions of the Prussian Chancellor Bismarck and the able strategic planning of General Helmuth von Moltke, Chief of the General Staff in Berlin, was born the great and powerful German Empire.

The Prussian attitude to warfare had been inspired earlier by the famous Prussian military writer General von Clausewitz (1780–1831). He had advocated that war should be total, aiming at the utter destruction of the enemy. "War," he said, "should be waged with the whole might of the national power." Two factors operating with increasing force during the latter part of the nineteenth century were to cause von Clausewitz's creed to be tacitly adopted not only by Prussia but by all the major European nations.

K. OF DENMARK

K. OF SWEDEN

NORTH SEA

BALTIC SEA

SCHLESWIG 1867 Joined Zollverein

HOLSTEIN 1867 Joined Zollverein

Lübeck

Hamburg

GR. D. OF OLDENBURG 1853 Joined Zollverein

Bremen

MECKLENBURG 1867 Joined Zollverein

1848–51 To German Confederation

K. OF THE NETHERLANDS

Rhine

KINGDOM OF HANOVER 1854 Joined Zollverein

NORTH

KINGDOM OF PRUSSIA

Elbe

Oder

Berlin

Vistula

GERMAN CONFEDERATION

RUSSIAN EMPIRE

1839 To German Confederation

K. OF BELGIUM

WALDECK 1838 Joined Zollverein

Elbe

1839 To Belgium

GR. D. OF LUXEMBOURG 1867 neutral.

D. OF NASSAU 1836 Joined Zollverein

K. OF SAXONY

1818 To German Confederation

1842–67 Part of German Zollverein

ALSACE-LORRAINE 1872 Joined Zollverein

GRAND DUCHY OF BADEN

K. OF

KINGDOM OF

K. OF FRANCE

Rhine

WÜRTTEMBERG 1836 Joined Zollverein

Danube

PR. OF HOHENZOLLERN

BAVARIA

Inn

AUSTRO-HUNGARIAN

SWITZERLAND

Danube

EMPIRE

Rhône

46°

K. OF SARDINIA

Sava

Drava

Boundary of German Confederation 1815–1866

Changes in boundary of German Confederation

Boundary of North German Confederation 1867

Boundary of German Empire 1871
In 1888 Boundary of German Zollverein (1834–88) is same as that of German Empire in 1871

Hanse Cities

Po

Miles   50   100   150   200   250

Kilometres   50 100   150   200   250   300   350   400

ADRIATIC SEA

© Geographical Projects

66

An infantryman of Washington's army
and a British soldier of the 38th
Regiment of Foot. The British soldier
was well drilled and well disciplined;
but he was less adaptable to unorthodox
tactics than his opponent, and his red
coat made him extremely conspicuous
on the field of battle.

finally defeated when her main force, under General Cornwallis,
surrendered at Yorktown, Virginia (1781).

Much of the Colonists' success, especially in the early stages of
the war, stemmed from their use of small bands of irregulars who
depended on speed and surprise and took maximum advantage
of cover and of their intimate knowledge of local terrain in
attacking and harassing British troops. Later there were other
important factors in the Colonists' favour. The French, still
smarting from their defeats in the Seven Years' War, began
secretly sending the Colonists money and supplies as early as
1776; and in 1778 they signed a treaty with the newly emerging
United States. Thereafter France sent an expeditionary force
whose officers were able to give sound advice on methods of
fortification, the use of artillery and European-style line of battle
formations. Perhaps even more important, Friedrich von Steuben,
a seasoned veteran of the Prussian army, became Inspector-
General of the American army in 1778 and, working closely with

Ulysses S. Grant

Robert E. Lee

its inspiring Supreme Commander, George Washington, quickly transformed it into a highly disciplined and efficient fighting force that more than matched the quality of Britain's own troops and foreign mercenaries.

But there were other reasons for Britain's failure. Her military leadership was poor and her centralized command, in London, too remote. Her troops, clad in their red coats, were too conspicuous in battle and too drilled in formal European battle tactics to match the more fluid and unorthodox methods of their opponents. And it took Britain too long to learn to respect the Americans' fighting ability and to stop despising their readiness to dig trenches—a practice they adopted as early as the Battle of Bunker Hill.

Just 80 years after the United States had assured their independence by the victory at Yorktown, and at a time when Europe was just settling down to the least war-torn half century in its history, came the most destructive and costly struggle ever

The decisive moment of the Battle of Gettysburg. It is the early afternoon of July 3, 1863, and the centre of the Federal line, firmly entrenched on a ridge, has received ample reinforcements. After a preliminary bombardment, Pickett now launches 15,000 Confederate troops in a do-or-die attack on the ridge. It is a gallant effort, but an effort doomed to failure.

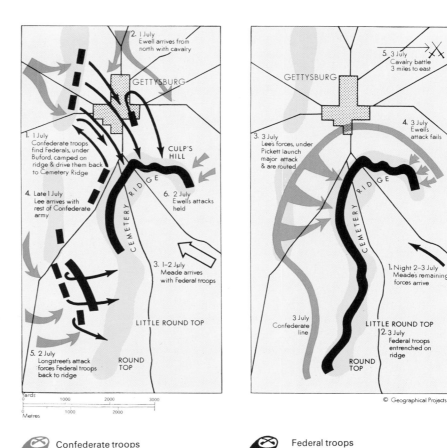

2. 1 July
Ewell arrives from north with cavalry

GETTYSBURG

CULP'S HILL

1. 1 July
Confederate troops find Federals, under Buford, camped on ridge & drive them back to Cemetery Ridge

4. Late 1 July
Lee arrives with rest of Confederate army

6. 2 July
Ewells attacks held

CEMETERY RIDGE

3. 1-2 July
Meade arrives with Federal troops

LITTLE ROUND TOP

5. 2 July
Longstreet's attack forces Federal troops back to ridge

ROUND TOP

Yards
0   1000   2000   3000
0   1000   2000
Metres

GETTYSBURG

5. 3 July
Cavalry battle 3 miles to east

3. 3 July
Lee's forces, under Pickett launch major attack & are routed

4. 3 July
Ewells attack fails

CEMETERY RIDGE

3 July
Confederate line

1. Night 2-3 July
Meades remaining forces arrive

2. 3 July
Federal troops entrenched on ridge

LITTLE ROUND TOP

ROUND TOP

© Geographical Projects

Confederate troops

Federal troops

Two stages in the Battle of Gettysburg. On July 1 Confederate troops find Buford's Federals encamped on high ground, and drive them back southeastwards to Cemetery Ridge. Meanwhile, Confederate cavalry under Ewell arrives and strikes southwards at Federals. Then, while Meade is arriving with Federal reinforcements, Lee comes on the scene with the rest of the Confederate army. On July 2, the Confederate right wing, under Longstreet, drives back the Federal left. The decisive moves come on July 3 (stage 2). By now Meade's remaining forces have arrived, and the Federals are firmly entrenched on Cemetery Ridge and high ground to the south of it. While a cavalry battle rages some distance to the east of Gettysburg, both Ewell and Pickett launch major attacks on the Federal lines, but both are repulsed.

fought in the New World—the American Civil War (1861–65). This conflict, precipitated by the secession of the 11 slave-holding southern states from the 23 northern states opposed to slavery, stands out in history as the first great "modern" war—the first major clash of arms to take place in the era of high industrialization.

The North (Federal States), led by Abraham Lincoln, was significantly stronger financially and industrially than the South (Confederate States), headed by Jefferson Davis; further, it had a population at least twice as great, and a white population at least four times as great. Thus, when the two sides first clashed at Fort Sumter in 1861, everything seemed in favour of the North. Yet such was the toughness and determination of the southerners that it took four years of bitter struggle and some 2,000 engagements large and small for the North to win the war.

It was war on a scale hitherto unknown, with battles being fought as far apart as the Atlantic seaboard and the plains to the west of the Mississippi, even though much of the fighting was

concentrated in the comparatively small but vital zone that embraced the northern capital, Washington, and the southern capital, Richmond, Virginia. And the new, advanced weapons employed—including magazine-loading rifles, manually operated machine guns, land mines, hand grenades and a variety of booby traps—helped to boost casualty figures on both sides to unprecedented levels.

The turning point of the war came in the summer of 1863, when Lee threw off the mainly defensive role the South had so far played and struck deep into the northern state of Pennsylvania with a Confederate force of some 75,000 men. From July 1 to July 3 that force clashed with a Federal army outnumbering it by almost three to two at Gettysburg. Three times Lee's forces attacked General Meade's Federals, who occupied high ground just to the south of the town—first their right, then their left, then their centre. Each attack was repulsed, with heavy losses on both sides, and eventually Lee's force was compelled to retreat. The South then had to resume a growingly hopeless defensive posture for the rest of the conflict.

Gettysburg produced some 44,000 casualties; and the cost in lives of the entire war was half a million. The use of advanced weaponry was certainly prominent among the reasons

American artillerymen of 1862, with an M-1857 "Napoleon," named after Napoleon III of France. This smooth-bore 12-pounder, first used in the United States in 1857, was favoured by both sides in the Civil War. Rifled hand guns had given the infantryman a temporary advantage at close quarters over artillerymen, whose guns were still smooth-bored. But the Napoleon, lighter than other guns of equal calibre, could hit back hard, spreading a hail of canister-shot that was devastating at a range of some 400 yards (365 metres).

for such heavy losses, but it was not the only one. The telephone and wireless telegraphy had not yet been invented; and relying on no better means of communication than flag- and lamp-signalling and the easily cut electric telegraph, even such great generals as Grant and Sherman on the northern side or Lee and Jackson on the southern side could not always exercise full control over the large and far-ranging armies at their command. Further, forces of such size could be brought into battle only by road or—better—by rail; and when, in mass, they reached the enemy position, they were often greeted with concentrated artillery fire before they had time to fan out and embark on flanking attacks.

This was the first major war in which mobility depended heavily on railroads and in which railroads were therefore used on the grand scale. Not only did the more industrially developed North have a larger rail network than the South, but the northern authorities also made more use of their railroads and organized them better for military purposes, making operations possible at points far distant from supply bases and enabling troops and equipment to be moved quickly right up to threatened sectors of the front. Hospital and armoured trains were introduced, and special corps were formed for the running and maintenance of the railroads.

Before the war ended, the Gatling gun was also in use. As the gunner turned a handle, its ten barrels rotated, and a complicated mechanism ensured that at any given instant five barrels were firing and ejecting their spent cartridges while the other five, which had just fired, were being reloaded.

REBELLION IN UPPER
& LOWER CANADA
1837
Britain v. settlers

RED RIVER REBELLION
1869–70
Government v. half-breeds

1812–14
U.S.A. v. Britain

AMERICAN CIVIL WAR
1861–65
Confederate States v. Federal States

MEXICAN WAR
1846–48
U.S.A. v. Mexico

SPANISH–AMERICAN WAR
1898
U.S.A. v. Spain

MEXICAN EXPEDITION
1861–67
France v. Mexico

1907
Honduras v. Nicaragua

WARS OF INDEPENDENCE
1816–22
Spain v Great Colombia

1865–71
Chile & Peru v. Spain

WAR OF INDEPENDENCE
1823–24
Spain v. Peru & Bolivia

WAR OF THE PACIFIC
1879–84
Chile v. Peru

1865–70
Argentina, Uru
& Brazil v. Para

1865–71
Chile & Peru v. Spain

1825–28
Argentina v. B

Another cardinal factor that made for the eventual victory of
the North was its superior naval strength. Its larger fleet of
steamboats gave it virtual control of the rivers—an important
advantage in a country where inland waterways were a vital
means of transport. And the more numerous sea-going ships of
the North were able to mount an effective blockade of the ports
of the South, thus stopping the economically essential export of
cotton to Europe. (Although Britain's cotton mills suffered badly,
Britain made no attempt to break the blockade.)

Yet important though railroads and ships were in the struggle,
it was not so much from them that American commanders
gradually learned new lessons, but from the appalling casualty
figures. In the later stages of the war, the heavy losses among the
hastily trained citizen troops dictated far-reaching changes in
tactics. Massed infantry formations, and shock cavalry attacks
against infantry armed with quick-firing weapons, were abandoned. Trenches, breastworks and rifle pits came into ever wider
use in defence against the increased deadliness of firepower; and
as a result the axe and the spade became essential items of the
infantryman's equipment.

*In the century that passed between the
end of the Napoleonic Wars and the outbreak of the First World War, there were
armed conflicts in every part of the
world except Antarctica. Even Australia
suffered an uprising in 1854—perhaps
the only instance of home warfare in its
history. But most of these wars were on
a small scale and in none of them did
the great powers of Europe show signs
of having learned what the American
Civil War could have taught them about
the waging of modern warfare.*

78

1864
[De]nmark v. Prussia & Austria

1ST & 2ND POLISH REVOLUTIONS
1830–31, 1863–64
Russia v. Poland

[BEL]GIAN REVOLUTION
[Belg]ium v. Netherlands

[FRAN]CO-PRUSSIAN WAR
1870–71
France v. Prussia

SEVEN WEEK'S WAR
1866
Austria v. Prussia

1859
[Fr]ance & Piedmont v. Austria

CRIMEAN WAR
1853–55
Britain, France & Turkey v. Russia

OCCUPATION OF PEKING
1859–60
Britain & France v. China

RUSSO-JAPANESE WAR
1904–05
Russia v. Japan

ITALIAN WAR OF INDEPENDENCE
1848–49
Piedmont & Naples v. Austria

RUSSO-TURKISH WARS
1828–29, 1875–78
Russia v. Turkey

1804–13, 1825–28
Persia v. Russia

BOXER RISING
1900–01
International force
(incl Britain, Germany) v. China

1897
Germany v. China

SINO-JAPANESE WAR
1894–95
Japan v. China

1832–34, 1835–37
1840–47
France v. Algeria

1ST & 2ND BALKAN WARS
1912–13
Bulgaria, Serbia &
Greece v. Turkey

AFGHAN WARS
1839–42, 1878–83
Britain v. Afghanistan

NORTH WEST FRONTIER
1849–90
Britain v. local tribes

TRIPOLITANIAN WAR
1911–12
Italy v. Turkey

1332–33,
1839–41
Egypt v.
Ottoman Empire

1856–57
Britain v. Persia

1ST BRITISH WAR
1840–42
Britain v. China

1882
Britain v. Egypt

SIKH WARS
1845–48, 1848–49
Britain v. Sikhs

1873–74
France v. Tonkin

SPANISH-AMERICAN WAR
1898–1902
U.S.A. v. Spain

CONQUEST OF SUDAN
1820–22
Egypt v. Sudan
1884–85, 1896–98
Britain & Egypt v. Sudan

1811–18
Egypt v. Wahabis

BURMESE WARS
1824–26, 1852–53, 1885
Britain v. Burma

ASHANTI WARS
1824–27, 1873–74,
1893–94, 1895–96
[Brit]ain v. Gold Coast

1895–96
Ethiopia v. Italy

1868
British expedition
to Abyssinia

SIAMESE CRISIS
1893
France v. Siam

DAHOMEY WARS
1840, 1842–44
France v. Dahomey

1875–76
Britain v. Perak

JAVANESE REVOLT
1825–30
Netherlands v. Java

1896
Britain v. Matabele & Mashona

1883–85, 1894–96
France v. the Hova

1808–40
Boers v. Zulus

ZULU WAR
1879
Britain v. Zulus

BOER WARS
1880–81, 1899–1901
Britain v. Boers

WAR OF THE AXE
1846–47
Britain v. Kaffirs

KAFFIR WAR
1877–78
Britain v. Kaffirs

EUREKA STOCKADE
1854
Government v. German
& Irish revolutionaries

2ND MAORI WAR
1860–70
Government v. Maoris

1ST MAORI WAR
1843–48
Settlers v. Maoris

© Geographical Projects

Although the European powers had observers and reporters on the spot in America, they failed to learn the lessons the Civil War could have taught them—in particular, that the sheer complexity and immensity of modern warfare had temporarily outstripped the means of controlling it. And for nearly half a century, apart from the short-lived Austro-Prussian War of 1866 and the Franco-Prussian War of 1870–71, Europe itself was to offer no battle-ground capable of reinforcing such lessons.

The many military adventures that Europe was involved in during the latter part of the nineteenth century were almost all small-scale imperial wars fought in distant lands. Britain fought battles in Egypt, Afghanistan, Persia, Bhutan, Ethiopia, West Africa, Zululand, the Sudan and various parts of India and China; and France had her limited colonial wars in North

Africa, West Africa and Indo-China. Yet none of these bore much more resemblance to full-scale modern war than did the long series of battles raging between Indians and white men in North America.

Britain did not again come up against a real military challenge until the Second South African War (1899–1902), better known as the Boer War. Then she found herself confronting—thousands of miles from home—a stubborn and determined enemy, fired with the spirit of a nation in arms. This, like the early stages of the American War of Independence, was largely a contest between orthodox forces trained in European methods of fighting and loosely organized irregulars. The British, like the Boers, were armed with magazine rifles, though of a different kind; but the Boers tended to be better marksmen and could fight equally well mounted or unmounted. Being of hardy farming stock, they could live off the land; and they were adept at guerrilla warfare. Further, they profited from the common British error of throwing into frontal attacks troops who were already exhausted from long marches. And finally, their artillery was doubtless superior to that of the British.

After a fairly even mixture of early failures and successes the British, under General Buller, were disastrously defeated at Spion Kop by the Boers' devastating rifle fire. Then, early in 1900, with the arrival of General Lord Roberts (sent to replace Buller) and his Chief of Staff, General Kitchener, the British took the offensive; and in a few months the main Boer forces were defeated. But the war was not finished. Kitchener, now left in charge by Roberts, had to contend with massive and prolonged guerrilla opposition, led by the Boer commander Christian de Wet. For many months continual raids and sabotage prevented Kitchener's 500,000-strong army from subduing the enemy force of less than 100,000. He then resorted to harsher methods, destroying Boer farms and confining the civil population in grim "concentration camps"—a sinister foreshadowing of the Nazi methods of 40 years later. Finally, to achieve victory, Kitchener had to parcel off the country into great barbed-wire enclosures and drive out the Boers area by area.

The years around the turn of the century witnessed two other wars of note. The Spanish-American War of 1898 was the first in which United States forces became involved overseas, and the Russo-Japanese War of 1904–5 was the first of modern times in which a European power suffered outright defeat at the hands of an Asian power.

Both conflicts were decided largely at sea. At the time of Wolfe's attack on Quebec, the British and French fleets had consisted wholly of wooden-walled sailing ships. Early on in the American Civil War the engagement fought between the Federal *Monitor* and the Confederate *Merrimac* had been the first clash between ironclads. But the advent of the torpedo-firing submarine around 1890 had, by the close of the nineteenth century, produced a revolution in naval construction. The need for greater armoured protection had rapidly led to the production of new-style battleships—heavily gunned, heavily armoured and,

Above: Boer irregulars, expert marksmen with Mauser rifles, in action at the Battle of Colenso, December 1899. In six days of that month three battles were fought. British losses totalled around 2000, but the Boers lost fewer than 200 men.

Below: Japanese battery near Port Arthur during the Russo-Japanese War. The successful siege of Russia's great Pacific naval base cost the Japanese 50,000 men; but it resulted in the destruction of the last remnant of Russia's vital Far Eastern fleet.

of course, powered solely by steam. And very soon had come first the small, swift destroyer, designed to counter the torpedo boat's threat to the battleship, and then the cruiser, intermediate in size between the battleship and the destroyer.

When war between Spain and the United States broke out in April 1898, the American navy, thoroughly up to date, was in a strong position to carry the fighting to Spain's overseas possessions, the Philippines and Cuba. Within a month four American cruisers, under the command of Admiral Dewey, had penetrated the defences of Manila Bay in the Philippines and destroyed an entire Spanish squadron. Then, in July, in Cuba, the Spanish suffered another reverse, when four of her armoured cruisers were sunk or disabled by an American battleship squadron while attempting to escape from Santiago harbour. By the end of July, following the successful American invasion of Puerto Rico, the war had been won, and the United States gained belated recognition as a world power.

The outcome of the Russo-Japanese War came as a stunning blow to Russia and a shock to the entire western world. It was not until 1854 that Japan had opened her doors to world trade and embarked on a programme of westernization. Then in the Sino-Japanese War of 1894–95, fought for control of Korea, she had heavily defeated the Chinese army and virtually destroyed the Chinese navy. Now, in 1904, Russia was trying to wrest control of Korea from Japan. Again the Japanese went to war, and again they won overwhelming victories.

First their navy attacked and bottled up Russia's eastern fleet in its main base—Port Arthur in Manchuria. Then they seized Dalny (now Lü-ta) preparatory to besieging and capturing Port Arthur, so that Russia's bottled-up eastern fleet could not be reinforced by Russian ships from the Baltic Sea. That siege was long and costly in lives, but by January 2, 1905, Port Arthur had surrendered. In May, when 32 somewhat antiquated Russian vessels eventually reached the Sea of Japan after a seven-month voyage from Europe, they were attacked by the Japanese fleet under Admiral Togo, and virtually annihilated at the two-day naval battle of Tsushima Strait. And meanwhile Russia had suffered severe military defeats along the Yalu river. By September, Russia had signed a treaty acknowledging Japan's supremacy in Korea and ceding certain territories to her.

This was more than a blow to the prestige of Tsarist Russia. It was also the beginning of the end of Europe's long overlordship of large areas of Asia. Nevertheless, like all the wars in which the European powers had been involved over the previous 50 years, the Russo-Japanese War was symptomatic of the expansionist fever that was intensifying national rivalries and producing an arms race of unprecedented dimensions. Soon only an "incident" was needed to spark off war on a gigantic scale.

That incident came in the Balkans in June 1914, when the Austrian Archduke Franz Ferdinand was assassinated at Sarajevo, in Bosnia, by Gavrillo Princip, a member of the Serbian terrorist organization "Union or Death," also called the "Black Hand," which was highly hostile to Austria.

7 Trench Warfare

A month after the Sarajevo incident the Austro-Hungarian Empire declared war on Serbia. Then came the chain reaction. Russia at once joined in to support Serbia, and Germany to support Austria. Next, because the French were known supporters of Russia, Germany declared war on France and on August 3 began moving troops towards France through Belgium. Next day Britain, treaty-bound to defend Belgian neutrality, entered the conflict on the side of France and Russia. By the end of August, Japan had declared war on Germany, and before the year closed Turkey was fighting on Germany's side. Soon Italy, Rumania and Portugal joined in on the French-British-Russian side (the Allies), and Bulgaria on the German-Austrian-Turkish side (the Central Powers). Much later, in April 1917, the United States entered the war against Germany.

This rightly named First World War was to cost more lives than any other in history. British dead numbered close to a million, French nearly 1,400,000, Russian 1,700,000, Austro-Hungarian 1,200,000 and German 1,800,000, and the total for all participants has been estimated at nearly 13 million. And in the course of the conflict three great empires were to fall: the Russian, the German and the Austrian.

The number of troops the leading belligerents put into action by mid-August 1914 is proof of their war-readiness. By that time Germany's fighting army totalled almost 1,900,000, Austria's 1,300,000, Russia's 1,300,000 and that of France nearly 1,200,000. Britain, without conscription, started with only 100,000.

Germany's initial strategy, aimed at avoiding war on two fronts simultaneously, was to leave much of the fighting with Russia to the Austrians for the time being, while her own armies gained a quick victory over France. This was to be achieved through a plan devised earlier by Count von Schlieffen. Since it seemed certain that France would concentrate her forces on her

German troops in action on the Western Front during the First World War— a scene of bursting shells, barbed wire and total devastation that was the common background of life for millions of men for the greater part of the conflict.

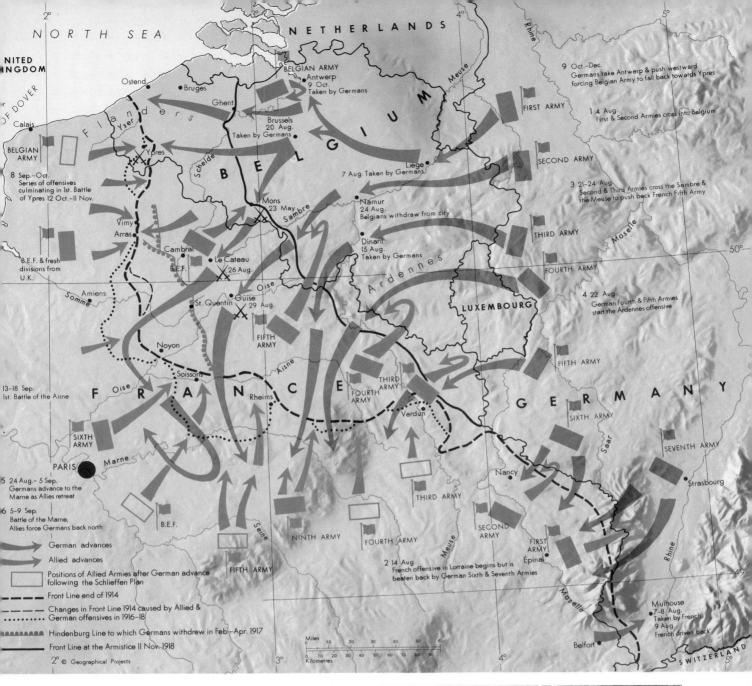

NORTH SEA

NETHERLANDS

UNITED KINGDOM

OF DOVER

Calais

BELGIAN ARMY

8 Sep.–Oct.
Series of offensives culminating in 1st Battle of Ypres 12 Oct.–11 Nov.

B.E.F. & fresh divisions from U.K.

13–18 Sep.
1st Battle of the Aisne

SIXTH ARMY

PARIS

5 24 Aug.– 5 Sep.
Germans advance to the Marne as Allies retreat

6 5–9 Sep.
Battle of the Marne, Allies force Germans back north

Ostend

Bruges

Ghent

Ypres

Vimy
Arras

Cambrai
B.E.F.

Amiens

Somme

St. Quentin   Guise
29 Aug.

Noyon

Soissons

Oise

FRANCE

B.E.F.

Seine

Le Cateau
26 Aug.

FIFTH ARMY

Aisne

Rheims

NINTH ARMY

FIFTH ARMY

BELGIAN ARMY
Antwerp
9 Oct. Taken by Germans

Brussels
20 Aug.
Taken by Germans

BELGIUM

Mons
23 May

Sambre

Namur
24 Aug.
Belgians withdraw from city

Dinant
15 Aug.
Taken by Germans

Liège
7 Aug. Taken by Germans

Ardennes

LUXEMBOURG

FOURTH ARMY

THIRD ARMY

Verdun

FOURTH ARMY

THIRD ARMY

SECOND ARMY

Meuse

2 14 Aug.
French offensive in Lorraine begins but is beaten back by German Sixth & Seventh Armies

Rhine

9 Oct.–Dec.
Germans take Antwerp & push westward forcing Belgian Army to fall back towards Ypres

1 4 Aug.
First & Second Armies cross into Belgium

3 21–24 Aug.
Second & Third Armies cross the Sambre & the Meuse to push back French Fifth Army

4 22 Aug.
German Fourth & Fifth Armies start the Ardennes offensive

FIRST ARMY

SECOND ARMY

THIRD ARMY

Moselle

FOURTH ARMY

FIFTH ARMY

GERMANY

SIXTH ARMY

Saar

SEVENTH ARMY

Nancy

Strasbourg

THIRD ARMY

SECOND ARMY

FIRST ARMY
Épinal

Moselle

Mulhouse
7–8 Aug.
Taken by French
9 Aug.
French driven back

Belfort

Rhine

SWITZERLAND

→ German advances

→ Allied advances

☐ Positions of Allied Armies after German advance following the Schlieffen Plan

▬ ▬ Front Line end of 1914

— ·· — Changes in Front Line 1914 caused by Allied & German offensives in 1916–18

······ Hindenburg Line to which Germans withdrew in Feb.–Apr. 1917

〰〰 Front Line at the Armistice 11 Nov. 1918

© Geographical Projects

Miles
0   10   20   30   40   50   60
0 10 20 30 40 50 60 70 80 90
Kilometres

A British gun battery in action at Cape Helles, Gallipoli, in 1915. The Gallipoli expedition went badly from the start, and proceeded from bad to worse. After a few months only one gun in this battery could still fire. The rest had broken down.

were occasionally to use deadly gases again, but seldom to much effect, because the prevailing westerly winds blew it back to their own lines, where it did as much damage as it did to the Allies.)

Several British statesmen had foreseen the continuing stalemate in the west and had advocated that the French be left to cope with the situation there while Britain attacked the enemy at some more vulnerable point. The idea was taken up, and the point eventually chosen was the Gallipoli peninsula. The objective was to force an entry of the Dardanelles, gateway to Constantinople, the Turkish capital, and gateway to the Bosphorus, through which help might be taken across the Black Sea to Russia.

The operation began as a purely naval one, but in March 1915, after four ships had struck mines, that phase ended, to be replaced the following month by a naval-military operation. The land campaign fared no better. The troops—largely Australians and New Zealanders (Anzacs)—gained only a foothold on the barren peninsula and, faced with a stubborn, determined Turkish defence, made virtually no progress in months of hard fighting. Indeed, much of the fighting again took the form of

Right: Map showing the alignment of European states in the First World War. States shown in green were neutral; those shown in grey were simply not involved. Apart from a small gap along the Danube, the Central Powers controlled an area stretching from the Persian Gulf to the North Sea. Allied territory included France and Britain to the west, Russia and Rumania to the east, Italy and Allied-held North Africa to the south. The Allies also had on their side Japan and, later, the United States.

Allied Powers in World War 1

Central Powers in World War 1

Neutral States

Miles

Kilometres

0° © Geographical Projects

trench warfare. The Anzacs' trials were aggravated by heat, flies, disease and water shortage, and in October the whole operation was called off. An imaginative attempt to find an alternative to the wasteful slogging match in France had failed.

In 1916, therefore, fighting on the Western Front was stepped up to reach its full fury, with each side mounting a huge offensive aimed at forcing a decision.

In February the Germans attacked on an eight-mile (13-kilometre) front against the French salient at Verdun, on the Meuse. Verdun, an historic French citadel ringed by a series of strong forts, was the traditional gateway into France for an enemy advancing from the east, and the Germans rightly calculated that the French would throw almost everything they had into its defence. Thus their intention was to "bleed France to death," leaving Britain that much easier to deal with.

In a battle lasting more than four months and contested by 15 or more divisions on each side, with both sides supported by guns firing several million shells, the hilly terrain before Verdun became a wilderness, and war plumbed new depths of horror. But although some of the outer forts fell, Verdun itself held. Three things enabled it to do so: the cool, inspiring leadership of the French commander, General Pétain; the heroic resistance of the troops; and France's brilliant handling of her supply problem. To supplement the inadequate rail communication from the south, only a single narrow road existed. And along that road, by a miracle of organization, poured a daily stream of 3,500 lorries carrying men and munitions to the front. No wonder the French called it "the Sacred Way."

By early July the German assault had petered out, and Verdun was saved. But for both sides the cost in casualties was prodigious: French 315,000, German 281,000.

Before the Verdun fighting ended, France and Britain had launched their own offensive, on the river Somme, over 100 miles to the northwest. From early July to mid-November the battle raged, resulting once more in little but carnage. On one day alone Britain lost nearly 60,000 men. In the entire battle Anglo-French casualties totalled some 600,000, and the German figure was around 450,000. Yet again defence had prevailed over attack and hopes of a breakthrough were shattered.

Nevertheless, the Battle of the Somme at least foreshadowed the possibility of breakthrough, because it was there that Britain first used a revolutionary new armoured vehicle—the tank. Designed to flatten down or cut through barbed-wire entanglements and to pass over shell holes as it went into action, it seemed capable of putting an end to trench warfare. But because it suffered teething troubles and because it was used only in insignificant numbers, it at first had little effect.

Late in 1916 there were changes in the high commands of both Germany and France. Hindenburg, who now became Chief of Staff of Germany's field armies, decided to shorten the German line on the Western Front, thus making it easier to defend in strength. For that purpose he withdrew from certain bulges, after

A scene of devastation after the Third Battle of Ypres (August–November, 1917). Over terrain like this, the risk of drowning ranked as yet another hazard of total war. Each side suffered some half a million casualties and the net result was an Allied gain of a mere handful of villages. Yet the derelict Mark IV tank in the picture serves as a reminder that at this very time the tank was about to come into its own, putting an end to the long and deadly stalemate of trench warfare.

utterly destroying the small areas evacuated, and established the stronger, shorter Hindenburg Line. General Nivelle, who succeeded Joffre as France's Commander in Chief, planned another great offensive towards the Aisne, between Soissons and Rheims, even though the shortening of Germany's line in that region had already lessened France's chance of victory. Nivelle raised the spirit of the French army—almost broken by Verdun—by virtually promising a quick end to the war if the new offensive succeeded. But the attack, launched in April 1917, failed miserably. In bitter reaction the French troops mutinied, and for a short time only a few divisions not tainted by revolt stood between Soissons and Paris.

For the Allies it was the war's most perilous moment. But the Germans, seemingly unaware of the mutiny, never attacked. The danger passed, and French morale was soon restored when Nivelle was dismissed and replaced by General Pétain.

Within two months of the collapse of Nivelle's offensive, the British under General Haig made a bid to widen the narrow Ypres salient, with the ultimate aim of pushing the enemy out of the Belgian ports, which were being used as submarine bases. In June they brilliantly captured the Messines ridge. But from August to November, as a further move to open the salient, there followed the Third Battle of Ypres (Passchendaele)—a campaign comparable in horror with Verdun. Under incessant rain the flat Flanders plain became a sea of mud, constantly churned up by shattering shell-fire. Every shell hole filled with water, and for troops struggling forward on slippery duckboards one slip could mean drowning. By the end of the campaign only Passchendaele ridge and a few villages had been gained. And the cost was some 500,000 casualties on each side.

A British Mark V tank, one of many used in the final battles of the First World War. It carries a fascine—a huge bundle of stakes that could be released to roll forwards and drop into an enemy trench, filling it sufficiently to let the tank cross it. The crewman's face is protected by a veil of chain mail.

This grim year, 1917, was also a momentous one in Russia. The war had gone increasingly badly for the ill-equipped, ill-organized Russian army from the start. A spectacular victory over the Austrians in mid-1916—under the outstanding general-ship of General Brusilov—had seemed to mark a turn of the tide. But the cost of achieving victory had proved too great for the Russian people. Suffering severely from food shortages and enormous manpower losses, they grew increasingly restive at the prospect of continuing the struggle and embarked on revolution.

The first outbreak, in March, left the Russians still fighting alongside France and Britain; but the second, in October, inspired by the dedicated communist leader Lenin, took her out of the war. Strategically this was a grave setback for the Western Allies. It enabled the Germans, using their first-rate railway system, to transfer more than 60 divisions to the west.

Nevertheless, 1917 offered the Allies two rays of hope. In April they had been joined by the United States, and although America had not yet put fighting troops into the field it was certain she would do so on a formidable scale in 1918. And in late November the British had scored their first notable success with tanks. At

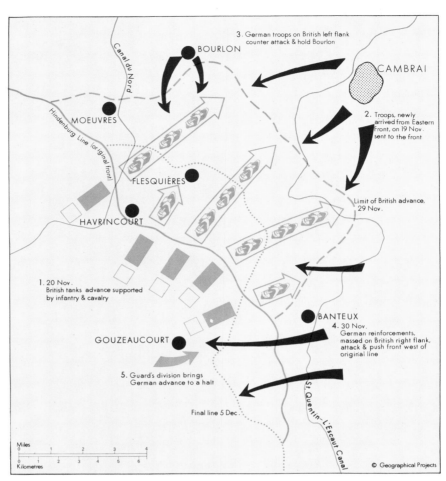

Right: Plan of the Battle of Cambrai. Late in 1917, following the collapse of the Russian war effort, it was clear that Germany would soon be able to bring massive reinforcements to the Western Front. The Allies therefore decided to launch an offensive at once. On November 20, British tanks, with infantry and cavalry support, broke through a six-mile (9.6-kilometre) section of the Hindenburg Line, and in nine days they advanced about four miles (6.2 kilometres) towards Cambrai. But already the Germans were able to bring to its defence troops newly arrived from Russia. Meanwhile, other German troops launched a counter-attack on the British left flank, and were thus able to hold Bourlon. And by December 5 a powerful German thrust against the British right wing had pushed part of the front back well to the west of where it stood before the battle began.

☐ British infantry

▨ British cavalry (guns)

🗦 British tank advances

➤ German advances

Below: Tanks, deployed in groups of three, go into action at the Battle of Cambrai. The cribs they carry are intended to be used as gap-fillers when crossing the very wide trenches of the Hindenburg Line.

Cambrai they deployed 350 of them on a six-mile (nine-kilo-metre) front and smashed through the enemy defences to advance six miles (nine kilometres) in a few hours.

By 1918 the demands of total war, in manpower, materials, transport and food, had so greatly depleted the resources of all the belligerents that they could not possibly carry on much longer, and it was the Germans, under the iron leadership of Hindenburg and Ludendorff, who now mustered all their remaining strength in an all-out bid for victory.

In March, along a 50-mile (80-kilometre) front around St. Quentin, they threw 40 divisions against the British, and made an advance of 40 miles (64 kilometres) in under a week. Hastily mustered French reserves helped to stem the advance, and almost at once General Foch was placed in over-all command of the Allied armies on the Western Front, to co-ordinate their efforts. In late May, in the Third Battle of the Aisne, the Germans attacked the French between Rheims and Soissons and drove them back to the Marne. In early July they attacked again, crossed the Marne and threatened Paris, as in 1914. But then Foch ordered a counter-attack, in which nine American divisions supported the French forces, and the Germans were quickly thrown back across the river.

They had reached the limit of their advance, exhausting the bulk of their remaining resources; and their gamble had failed.

Now began the Allied counter-offensive. Co-ordinated by Foch, it forced a long, desperate fighting retreat on the German army and ended in its eventual defeat. The Armistice was signed on November 11, 1918.

A major weakness in the German army had been its lack of armoured mobility. In no single battle did it ever employ more than 13 tanks, whereas Britain alone employed hundreds, not only at Cambrai but also at the Battle of Amiens, in August 1918. There, more than 400 heavy tanks, supported by aircraft, swept forward with the infantry to breach the German lines and deliver a shattering blow at the already faltering enemy.

The long war had raged worldwide. Turkey had done battle with the British (whose Colonel T. E. Lawrence had galvanized the Arabs into active revolt against the Turks) in Egypt, Palestine and Mesopotamia; Allied forces had fought against Germany and Austria in the Balkans, to assist Serbia; the Italians, in the north of their own land, had battled against Austrian and German troops; in Africa, Germany had been forced to defend her possessions—Togoland, the Cameroons and German East Africa —against both Britain and France; and in New Guinea and the remote Bismarck Archipelago, German colonists had fought with Australian and New Zealand forces. Yet in essence the war was decided on the Western Front, as French militarists had predicted from the start.

At sea there was only one major engagement—the Battle of Jutland, in which the British and German fleets clashed in May 1916. Although it was scarcely decisive, the German High Seas Fleet never again ventured out to face the British Grand Fleet. Far more telling was the battle fought under the seas. With their deadly new submarine craft, the U-boat, the Germans set out to counter the crippling naval blockade that Britain had imposed on them. So ferocious was their attack on all shipping supplying Britain's vital necessities, including food, that by the spring of 1917 the sinkings had brought Britain to the verge of starvation. Only the introduction of the convoy system, the use of depth-charges and tighter rationing saved her.

Not only did this war take to the sea depths but also—for the first time—to the air. From the start German ships employed airships for spotting; and in January 1915 a zeppelin—the great rigid airship earlier devised by Count von Zeppelin—first appeared over England, dropping a few bombs on East Anglia. It achieved nothing of military importance, but it marked the moment when civilians were first subjected to air bombardment.

The unwieldy airship was soon outmatched by the airplane. At first it was used for reconnaissance and as a fighter for local use over trenches. But when it was equipped with a machine gun, the concept of air support for ground troops gradually developed, and the plane was used in that way not only on the Western Front but also in other theatres of war, including Palestine. The bomber, too, emerged; when its range increased, the German Gotha was able to raid London; and in 1917 seven British Camel bombers took off on a raid from the converted battle cruiser *Furious*, making it the first operational aircraft carrier.

In the early days of the First World War the airplane was little used except for reconnaissance. By 1918 it had already become an essential weapon of war. German bombers, especially, had considerable range and power. Above are a British Sopwith Camel fighter and a German Staaken giant bomber, together with silhouettes of both, drawn to the same scale. The Sopwith had a wing span of 28 feet (8.5 metres). The Staaken, with a span of 138 feet (42 metres), was capable of carrying a four-ton bomb load.

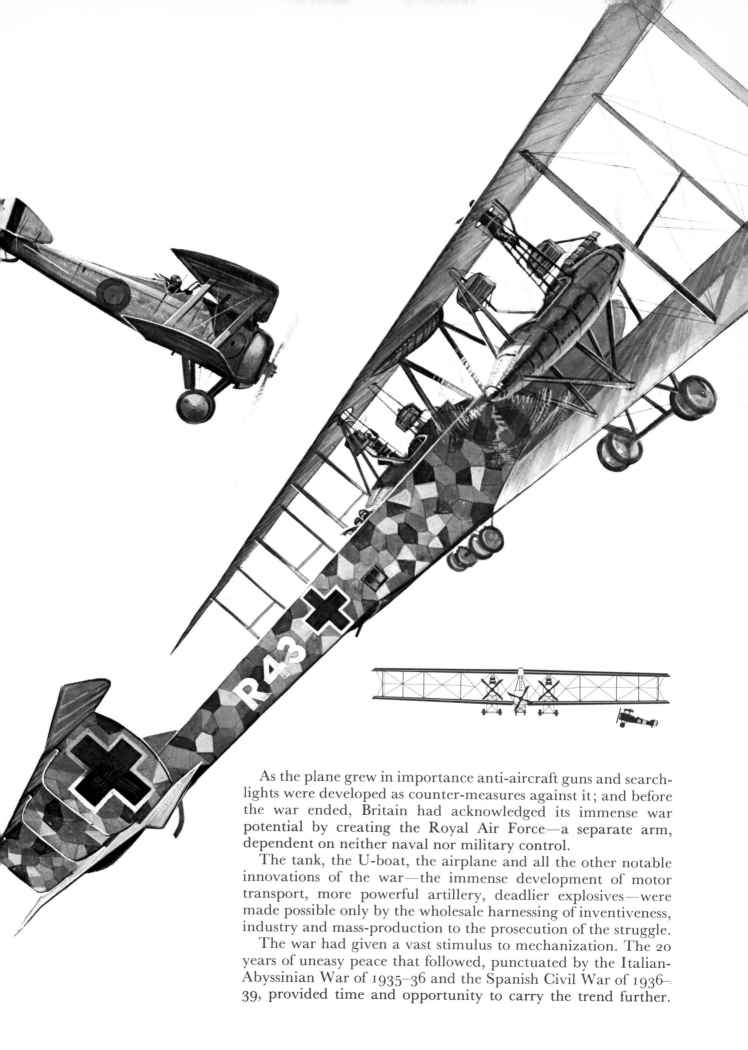

As the plane grew in importance anti-aircraft guns and search-lights were developed as counter-measures against it; and before the war ended, Britain had acknowledged its immense war potential by creating the Royal Air Force—a separate arm, dependent on neither naval nor military control.

The tank, the U-boat, the airplane and all the other notable innovations of the war—the immense development of motor transport, more powerful artillery, deadlier explosives—were made possible only by the wholesale harnessing of inventiveness, industry and mass-production to the prosecution of the struggle.

The war had given a vast stimulus to mechanization. The 20 years of uneasy peace that followed, punctuated by the Italian-Abyssinian War of 1935–36 and the Spanish Civil War of 1936–39, provided time and opportunity to carry the trend further.

8 Mechanized Warfare

To those who lived through it, the First World War seemed the ultimate in total warfare. Yet the Second World War, which began in September 1939, carried the concept of totality significantly further. Before it had ended there were fighting fronts all over the globe; industrial, scientific, technological and manpower resources were almost everywhere strained to breaking point; and in a score of lands civilians found themselves no less in physical danger than were the fighting men.

Above all, this was to be a war of mechanization. Military innovation and invention had been at work steadily since 1918, and as the Second World War itself gained impetus their pace was stepped up. As a result a host of new weapons and new devices were to be employed. Among them were machine guns far lighter than those of 1918; faster-firing artillery pieces; rockets and rocket launchers; speedy, heavily gunned tanks equipped with radio-telephones and having a range of up to 200 miles (320 kilometres); jet propulsion; the proximity fuse; the RDX explosive, almost twice as powerful as TNT; radar and a wide range of electronic equipment for communications.

Yet it was one single element that utterly transformed the face of war: air power, which when used in support of armoured attack made nonsense of old ideas of static linear defence.

Not only were aircraft larger, faster and more powerfully armed than those of 1914–18, but they were also employed in greater numbers and a greater variety of ways. They were used for intelligence, reconnaissance, aerial photography and mapping. They were called on to move men, munitions and fuel swiftly to danger points and to drop paratroopers behind enemy lines. Bombers with fighter support hammered military targets deep

The scene is northern France in the summer of 1944. For three years Hitler has been master of all western Europe except Spain and Portugal. Now these American Sherman tanks, supported by British Spitfire Mark IX fighters, form part of a vast Allied mechanized force that is beginning to thrust the German army back towards the Rhine.

96

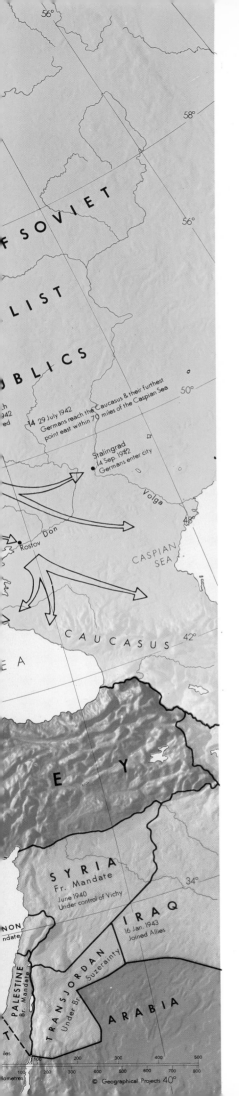

Above: Triumphal progress of German tanks in Poland. They are part of a quite small armoured group that had wiped out an entire Polish battalion southwest of Danzig.

France, they then reached the Channel coast in a matter of days, trapping and cutting off the Allied forces in Belgium. The vaunted Maginot Line had not even been tested. Instead, its northern extremity had simply been turned.

For the Allies the outcome was devastating. The Belgians were forced to surrender; and as the Germans turned southwards, the disorganized and demoralized French army was crushingly defeated. The great bulk of Britain's 250,000-strong Expeditionary Force, having made a fighting retreat to the beaches of Dunkirk, was miraculously rescued by a vast fleet of small boats; but nearly all the expedition's equipment had to be abandoned.

Britain, now standing alone, faced the imminent prospect of a German invasion. But an essential prerequisite to it was the destruction of Britain's Royal Air Force, and this, despite massive and sustained attacks, the German Luftwaffe failed to achieve. The year-long battle that raged in the skies over Britain proved that the air dimension was now decisive in warfare.

While those air battles still raged, Britain was contending with another threat. The Italians, who then controlled Libya,

Left: The widespread successes of German arms in the early stages of the Second World War and the resultant line-up of European states at the end of 1941. Britain then stood alone against Hitler in the west. In the east his troops were advancing deep into Russia and in North Africa they had reached the Egyptian border.

had entered the war on Germany's side just before the fall of France. Three months later, in September 1940, Libyan-based Italian troops invaded Egypt, posing a threat to the Suez Canal, vital to Britain's sea traffic with the East. By the following January, British troops had reversed the position and invaded Libya. But Britain's success was short-lived. In April 1941 a joint Italian-German force, brilliantly led by Germany's General Rommel, pushed the British back to the Egyptian frontier.

For the next 18 months the western desert, almost devoid of civilian population and imposing immensely long lines of communication on armies, was a classic scene of mechanized warfare. In terrain ideal for armoured operations, opposing tank formations moved back and forth across the desert like fleets of ships at sea, their supplies provided by air or motorized transport. By the close of 1941, Britain had thrust Rommel's forces back again; then in May 1942, in his second offensive, Rommel advanced to within 70 miles of Alexandria; finally, starting from El Alamein in October 1942, the British Eighth Army under the command of General Montgomery chased Rommel's Afrika Korps right out of Libya into Tunisia. Only the fact that Britain held Malta, and so kept open her Mediterranean supply line, made this great advance possible.

Nevertheless, in the spring of 1941 Germany unquestionably held the upper hand in North Africa. By that time she had also registered success after success in the Balkans. In October 1940 her troops had marched into Rumania, partly to protect the invaluable Rumanian oilfields from British air attack and

Two of the leading contestants in the struggle between Britain's R.A.F. and the German Luftwaffe—a Hawker Hurricane Mark I fighter and a Junkers JU87B "Stuka" dive-bomber. The Hurricane is said to have shot down more German planes than all other British fighters combined. The "Stuka," supreme among Germany's dive-bombers, was fitted with sirens that set up a blood-curdling howl as it dived to the attack.

partly to keep them out of the hands of the Russians, who had recently occupied part of Rumania. Then, in April 1941, Hitler had added Yugoslavia and Greece to his conquests.

But by now Russia was bitterly blaming Germany for spreading the war; and Hitler feared that all his victories might count for little if that bitterness flared into armed hostility. He decided to act first. In June 1941, tearing up Germany's non-aggression pact with Russia, he launched a great eastern offensive with 120 divisions on a 2,000-mile (3,200-kilometre) front.

Germany hoped to knock Russia out by a swift, overwhelming blitzkrieg, and at first she seemed likely to succeed. By December, having encircled huge pockets of Russian troops in a three-pronged attack, the Germans had besieged Leningrad, penetrated the Crimean peninsula and the Don valley and reached the outskirts of Moscow. But that, for the time, was the limit of their advance. Then, fighting off a vigorous Russian counter-offensive, the Germans suffered the rigours of a winter campaign for which they were wholly unprepared.

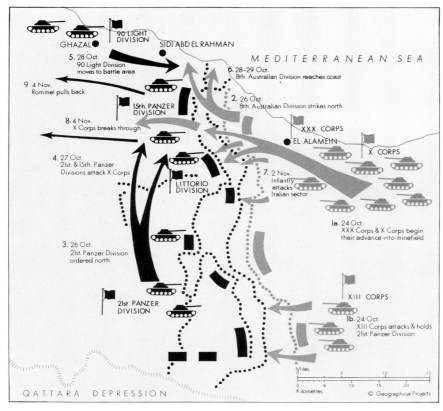

A plan of the battle.

MEDITERRANEAN SEA

GHAZAL ●
90 LIGHT DIVISION
SIDI ABD EL RAHMAN

5. 28 Oct.
90 Light Division
moves to battle area

6. 28–29 Oct.
8th. Australian Division reaches coast

9. 4 Nov.
Rommel pulls back

15th. PANZER
DIVISION

2. 26 Oct.
8th. Australian Division strikes north

8. 4 Nov.
X Corps breaks through

XXX CORPS

● EL ALAMEIN

X CORPS

4. 27 Oct.
21st. & 15th. Panzer
Divisions attack X Corps

LITTORIO
DIVISION

7. 2 Nov.
Infantry
attacks
Italian sector

Ia. 24 Oct.
XXX Corps & X Corps begin
their advance into minefield

3. 26 Oct.
21st. Panzer Division
ordered north

21st. PANZER
DIVISION

XIII CORPS

Ib. 24 Oct.
XIII Corps attacks & holds
21st Panzer Division

Miles   5   10   15
0
Kilometres   5   10   15   20

QATTARA DEPRESSION

© Geographical Projects

Left: A plan of the battle. The first blow was struck on October 24, when Montgomery's left armoured wing attacked and held the German 21st Panzer Division near the all-but-impassable Qattara Depression. Then his right wing began clearing mines and advancing through the minefield that had been laid to prevent an Allied advance along the coast, where supplies could be brought in by sea. Within two days the German left was so seriously threatened that the 21st Panzer Division was ordered north to relieve the pressure on it. By the end of October the Allied forces had reached the coast at Sidi Abd el Rahman.

By November 4 the Allies had achieved a complete breakthrough and Rommel had begun the long retreat to the west. Six months later, American and British troops were able to capture hundreds of thousands of German and Italian prisoners in Tunisia.

Allied armour

Allied infantry

Western edge of Allied minefield

Axis armour

Axis infantry

Axis minefields

In the summer of 1942, Germany renewed her onslaught, concentrating on the southern section of the front. By mid-August, in quest of desperately needed oil, Hitler's troops reached the Caucasus and, farther north, advanced on Stalingrad (now Volgograd), on the Volga. The Battle of Stalingrad produced the bitterest fighting of the whole Russo-German conflict—and the worst German reverse. As winter approached, the besieged Russians, forced into a contracting circle, were resisting fanatically street by street, and facing what seemed certain defeat. But by November, Russia had mounted a massive counter-offensive, planned and led by Marshal Zhukov, among the greatest commanders on any front. This counter-attack threatened to envelop the besieging German force in a vast pincer movement, and the only sensible recourse for the Germans was withdrawal. But Hitler refused to allow this, and on February 2, 1943, after enduring appalling privations, the remnants of the German Sixth Army under General Paulus were forced to surrender.

From that moment, which coincided roughly with the chasing of Rommel's army from Libya into Tunisia, the tide of war steadily turned against Germany.

Just over a year earlier, the war had been vastly extended. Up to the end of 1941 it had been confined to Europe, Africa and the Near East—not forgetting the Atlantic, where German submarines were waging a ruthless battle against Allied merchant shipping. Then in December 1941, without any declaration of war, Japanese ships and planes launched a surprise attack on the United States base at Pearl Harbor in the Hawaiian Islands, sinking and damaging many naval vessels. Within four days America was at war not only with Japan but with Germany and Italy too; and Britain had declared war on Japan.

Throughout the 1930s, Japan had waged frequent campaigns in Manchuria and China, seizing huge territories and building up what she called a "Greater East Asia Co-prosperity Sphere." This she aimed to protect by creating a broad defensive barrier of additional mainland territory and Pacific islands. Simultaneously

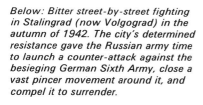

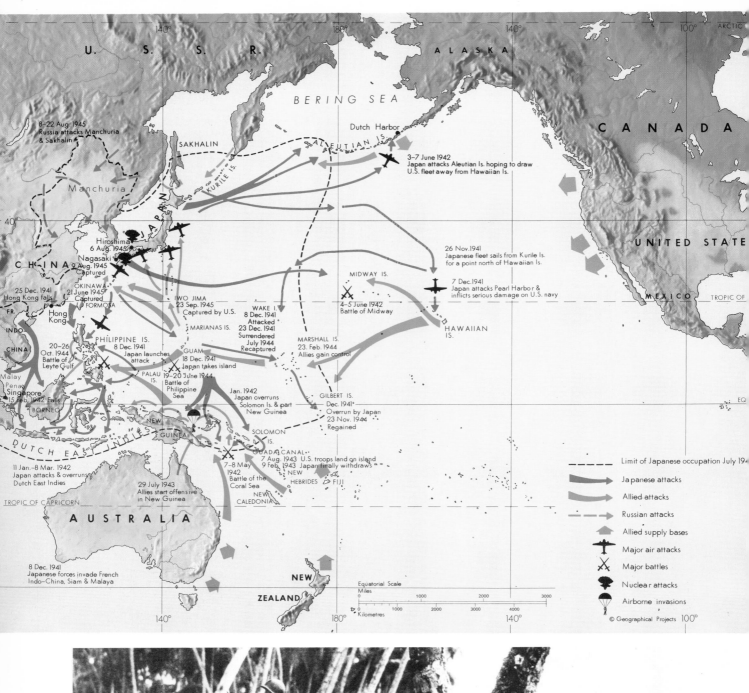

8–22 Aug. 1945
Russia attacks Manchuria & Sakhalin

BERING SEA

U.S.S.R.

SAKHALIN

KURILE IS.

ALEUTIAN IS.

Dutch Harbor

ALASKA

CANADA

3–7 June 1942
Japan attacks Aleutian Is. hoping to draw U.S. fleet away from Hawaiian Is.

Manchuria

JAPAN

Hiroshima
6 Aug. 1945

Nagasaki
9 Aug. 1945
Captured

OKINAWA
21 June 1945
Captured

FORMOSA

CHINA

25 Dec. 1941
Hong Kong falls

Hong Kong

FR.

INDO-

CHINA

IWO JIMA
23 Sep. 1945
Captured by U.S.

MARIANAS IS.

WAKE I.
8 Dec. 1941
Attacked
23 Dec. 1941
Surrendered
July 1944
Recaptured

MIDWAY IS.

4–5 June 1942
Battle of Midway

26 Nov. 1941
Japanese fleet sails from Kurile Is. for a point north of Hawaiian Is.

7 Dec. 1941
Japan attacks Pearl Harbor & inflicts serious damage on U.S. navy

HAWAIIAN IS.

UNITED STATE

MEXICO

TROPIC OF

PHILIPPINE IS.
8 Dec. 1941
Japan launches attack

GUAM
18 Dec. 1941
Japan takes island

MARSHALL IS.
23 Feb. 1944
Allies gain control

20–26
Oct. 1944
Battle of
Leyte Gulf

PALAU
IS.

19–20 June 1944
Battle of
Philippine
Sea

Jan. 1942
Japan overruns
Solomon Is. & part
New Guinea

GILBERT IS.
Dec. 1941
Overrun by Japan
23 Nov. 1944
Regained

Malay
Penin.

Singapore
15 Feb. 1942 Falls

BORNEO

NEW
GUINEA

SOLOMON
IS.

GUADALCANAL
7 Aug. 1943 U.S. troops land on island
9 Feb. 1943 Japan finally withdraws

EQ

DUTCH EAST INDIES

11 Jan.–8 Mar. 1942
Japan attacks & overruns
Dutch East Indies

29 July 1943
Allies start offensive
in New Guinea

7–8 May
1942
Battle of the
Coral Sea

NEW
HEBRIDES

FIJI

NEW
CALEDONIA

TROPIC OF CAPRICORN

AUSTRALIA

8 Dec. 1941
Japanese forces invade French
Indo–China, Siam & Malaya

NEW
ZEALAND

Equatorial Scale
Miles
0   1000   2000   3000

0   1000   2000   3000   4000
Kilometres

Limit of Japanese occupation July 194

Japanese attacks

Allied attacks

Russian attacks

Allied supply bases

Major air attacks

Major battles

Nuclear attacks

Airborne invasions

© Geographical Projects

Left: Main events in the Pacific theatre of war, from Japan's attack on Pearl Harbor in December 1941 to the dropping of atomic bombs on Hiroshima and Nagasaki in August 1945. From start to finish, the United States navy fought unceasingly, its submarines taking a constant toll of Japanese shipping, its plane-carrying surface ships hitting hard at Japan's navy and air bases. The battles of the Coral Sea, Midway Island and Leyte Gulf rank among the greatest naval actions of all time.

Below, left: Starting the all-out drive against the Japanese in the South Pacific, July 1943. American troops establishing a beach-head on Rendova Island, in the Solomons.

with the Pearl Harbor attack, therefore, she invaded the Philippines and the Malay peninsula, where she inflicted on the British one of the most humiliating defeats in their history, by the rapid capture of the great naval base of Singapore.

The successes at Pearl Harbor and Singapore gave Japan temporary local superiority in sea and air power. And with this advantage she was quickly able to seize the Dutch East Indies and Burma. In the latter country, the comparatively raw British-Indian forces were routed in a matter of weeks by seasoned Japanese troops who had served in Manchuria and China and who were also thoroughly trained in jungle warfare. These victories provided Japan with prodigious sources of the raw materials and manpower needed for a prolonged struggle.

Meanwhile, in this now truly global conflict, the Americans and Japanese faced each other across the vast expanse of the Pacific. America's only way to dislodge her adversaries from the myriad islands they had occupied was by first fighting and defeating them at sea. And the sea struggle of the Pacific was one of the most difficult, and hardest fought, of the entire war.

Although it should not be forgotten that American submarines played a vital role in this struggle, sinking huge numbers of Japanese ships, it was the great sea battles that settled many issues. The battles of the Coral Sea (May 1942), Midway Island (June 1942) and Leyte Gulf (October 1944), all won by America, made naval history. In each of them air power, in the form of aircraft launched from carriers, was far more decisive than naval guns. So great was the striking range of planes compared with that of guns that the Battle of the Coral Sea (which prevented a possible Japanese invasion of Australia) was fought entirely by carrier-borne aircraft, the opposing fleets scarcely sighting each other. Midway (which stopped Japanese expansion into the central Pacific) was also essentially a battle of naval planes. And in the Battle of Leyte Gulf (which forced the Japanese to withdraw from Philippine waters, leaving the way free for American troops to complete the reconquest of the islands), Japanese pilots, using *kamikaze* tactics, sank or damaged 23 American vessels by crashing their bomb-laden planes onto them.

Nevertheless, by the time the Battle of Leyte Gulf was fought, America had clearly wrested air superiority from Japan. And in the West, the Allies had already wrested it from Germany.

In 1940–41, even though German planes failed to gain the mastery of Britain's skies, they were able—almost with impunity—to bomb British cities indiscriminately by night. By mid-1942, starting with two 1,000-bomber night raids on Cologne and Essen, Britain had already begun the strategic bombing of industrial targets in Germany. The losses were at first high and the results unimpressive. But soon, with the introduction of four-engined Lancaster and Halifax bombers and more powerful bombs, German industry began to feel the pinch. Then, while the R.A.F. night campaign still continued, the United States Air Force, operating from bases in Britain, joined in with massive daylight raids by Flying Fortresses—and later B-29 Superfortresses—escorted to their distant targets by long-range Mustang fighters. Major damage was now inflicted on German industry, notably the aircraft industry, helping to increase the Allies' air superiority still further.

Yet Allied air supremacy alone could not win the war. That could be done only by an all-out invasion by land, sea and air across the English Channel. And as 1943 drew to a close, the opportune moment was clearly near at hand.

During that year the Russians—who had so far borne by far the greater part of the land fighting against Germany, sustaining many millions of casualties in the process—won the Battle of Kursk, the greatest tank battle of the war. They then broke the 16-month siege of Leningrad and drove the German army back almost to the Ukraine. In March of the same year the Americans,

In November 1942 Germany started to lose ground around Stalingrad just as Rommel's force began its retreat from El Alamein. From then on the tide of war flowed strongly against Hitler. The arrows showing Allied advances tell their own tale. Starting from Egypt, Casablanca, Russia and France, they finally converge in the heart of Germany.

who had earlier captured French North Africa in a great amphibious operation, advanced eastwards into Tunisia. There they linked up with British forces advancing westwards from Libya. By mid-May the joint Allied armies had captured hundreds of thousands of German and Italian prisoners and put an end to the resistance of the Axis powers in Africa.

Two months later, United States, Canadian and British forces successfully invaded Sicily. In early September they crossed the Strait of Messina into southern Italy; and the Italians, whose dictator, Mussolini, had recently resigned, immediately signed an armistice—although German troops long continued fighting the Allies in Italy.

In 1943 then, the date of the great invasion was fixed—for the late spring of 1944. Named "Overlord," it was to be the biggest combined land, sea and air operation in the history of warfare. Its aim was to land a powerful Allied force, supported by airborne troops, on five French beaches between the eastern flank of the Cotentin peninsula and the area just north of Caen. The supreme commander was to be America's General Eisenhower, with Britain's General Montgomery commanding the Allied ground forces.

By the early months of 1944, Britain had become a vast military camp and arsenal. Its harbours sheltered more than 4,000 naval vessels and a host of landing craft. Its airfields held some 15,000

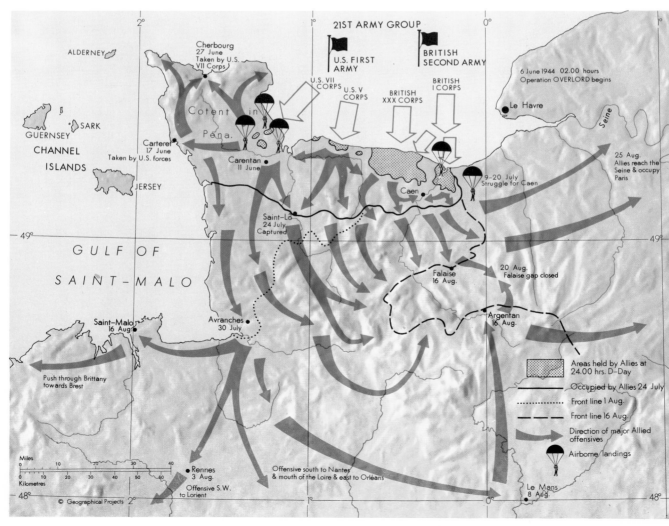

21ST ARMY GROUP

U.S. FIRST ARMY

BRITISH SECOND ARMY

6 June 1944 02.00 hours
Operation OVERLORD begins

ALDERNEY

Cherbourg
27 June
Taken by U.S.
VII Corps

U.S. VII CORPS

U.S. V CORPS

BRITISH XXX CORPS

BRITISH I CORPS

Le Havre

GUERNSEY

SARK

CHANNEL ISLANDS

JERSEY

Cotentin Pena.

Carteret
17 June
Taken by U.S. forces

Carentan
11 June

Caen

9-20 July
Struggle for Caen

25 Aug.
Allies reach the
Seine & occupy
Paris

Saint-Lô
24 July
Captured

GULF OF SAINT-MALO

Falaise
16 Aug.

20 Aug.
Falaise gap closed

Argentan
16 Aug.

Saint-Malo
16 Aug.

Avranches
30 July

Push through Brittany
towards Brest

Areas held by Allies at
24.00 hrs. D-Day

Occupied by Allies 24 July

Front line 1 Aug.

Front line 16 Aug.

Direction of major Allied
offensives

Airborne landings

Miles
0   10   20   30   40
0 10 20 30 40 50 60
Kilometres

© Geographical Projects

Rennes
3 Aug.

Offensive S.W.
to Lorient

Offensive south to Nantes
& mouth of the Loire & east to Orleans

Le Mans
8 Aug.

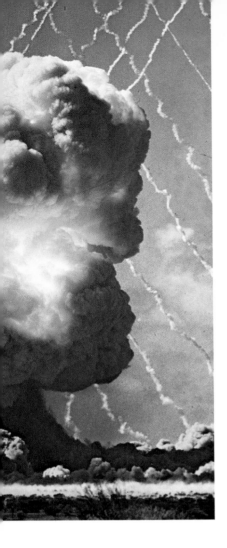

Above: An atom bomb explosion of the kind that wrought havoc in Hiroshima and Nagasaki in August 1945. (Here the grid system appearing as a background is used to measure the magnitude of the explosion.) The advent of nuclear weapons brought the Second World War to a sudden end, but it also set problems that have remained to plague the world ever since.

Left: Operation "Overlord," the biggest combined land, sea and air operation in history, began on June 6, 1944. Early that day, American, British and Commonwealth troops were landed on five beaches a little to the east of the Cotentin Peninsula. Before the end of the month they had captured most of the peninsula. By the end of July they had begun to fan out in all directions and had pivoted around and taken Caen. Before August ended they had reached the Seine and liberated Paris.

aircraft of all kinds. Its camps and barracks bulged with 17 divisions of sea- and air-borne invasion troops, backed by a huge follow-up force. The accompanying array of armour, transport and artillery was colossal. Inventive genius had been called in to produce, among other devices, "swimming tanks" that could fire from the sea's edge even before the first infantry landed, and two enormous prefabricated harbours, called "mulberry harbours," to be towed across the Channel to provide for the landing of stores and equipment. And PLUTO—short for Pipe Line Under the Ocean—was laid to carry petrol to the assault areas.

The outstanding features of the whole gigantic operation were the secrecy, organization and meticulous planning that preceded it, and the close Anglo-American and inter-service liaison that prevailed throughout. Added to these, the R.A.F. had earlier mounted massive preliminary attacks on France's coastal defences—Hitler's vaunted "Atlantic Wall"—as well as on the rail network of northern France. Yet despite all this, the difficulties that faced the invaders when they first went in, on June 6, were formidable. On some beaches there was much bloody fighting against tough enemy opposition for several days.

But very soon the invaders had established a firm footing in France. And French resistance fighters (who, like the freedom fighters in every country Hitler had invaded, had long been working under cover for the Allied cause) quickly emerged into the open to help them. Steadily the Allies pushed forwards, and by the end of August Paris had been liberated. Hitler, who had earlier launched his V-1s (flying bombs) on southern England, now unleashed a barrage of V-2s (long-range rockets with heavy warheads). But their military effect was nil, and the Allied armies pressed on relentlessly towards the German frontier.

Meanwhile the Russians, still on the offensive, had continued sweeping rapidly westwards, and by the end of February 1945 they were within 40 miles of Berlin. The Germans, now threatened from two sides and with their homeland under constant Anglo-American air attack, found themselves staring defeat in the face. In March, Eisenhower's force crossed the Rhine; at the end of April the Americans linked up with the Russians on the Elbe; and on May 7, with Hitler dead in the ruins of Berlin, Germany surrendered unconditionally on all fronts.

The war in the West was over, but there still remained Japan, now under ruthless assault by the Americans in the Pacific and by the Allies in Burma. At the expense of many months—perhaps years—of further fighting, she might well have been defeated with conventional weapons. But the Allies were weary, and in this war in which science had already played so great a part, scientists now offered a short cut to victory. On August 6, 1945, the first atom bomb to be exploded in anger was dropped on Hiroshima. Three days later the second one was dropped on Nagasaki. On August 14, Japan, too, surrendered unconditionally.

Nobody regretted the end of the war, but the manner in which it ended has weighed on the world's conscience ever since. And the advent of nuclear weapons has set problems that have ever since plagued the world in peace and war alike.

9 Recent Warfare

As the Second World War drew to a close, Allied statesmen planned to replace the old League of Nations, which had failed in its aim "to achieve international peace and security," with a new and more effective body. That new body—the United Nations Organization—came into existence in October 1945. The aims of UNO were similar to those of the League, but it soon came to embrace a wider membership, which this time included both the United States and Russia. Furthermore, the new organization quickly empowered itself to set·up a United Nations army, composed of troops from member states, to carry out "police" action against any offending state.

UNO has unquestionably had its successes, preventing a number of armed conflicts and limiting the scope of certain others. Yet the years since 1945 have probably witnessed at least as many wars as any other 30-year period in history. Why? There are two major reasons: a world clash of ideologies, and a strong upsurge of nationalism in lands long subjected to colonial rule.

The clash of ideologies began almost as soon as the Second World War ended, and produced the "Cold War"—the long period of mutual distrust and fear between Russia on the one hand and the Western Allies on the other.

The only reason why communist Russia had been an ally of the Western Powers in the fight against Hitler was that she had been attacked by Germany. East and West then became united in one thing only—their determination to defeat the German aggressor. Once this was achieved, the community of interests ceased abruptly, and Russia felt free to resume her long-standing ideological campaign against the world's major capitalist powers. On the passive side, this meant non-cooperation with her co-victors. On the active side, it meant spreading communist propaganda and communist influence by every means short of full-scale war. Such means included subversion, sabotage, the

Throughout the ages, new methods of attack have called into being effective new methods of defence. One answer to today's highly manoeuvrable supersonic military planes is this Rapier anti-aircraft missile system. In daylight the operator tracks the moving target visually. A computer first signals when a missile must be fired, then guides it along the optical sight line to the target. Equipped with an "add-on radar," the Rapier operates with equal effectiveness in the dark.

direct or indirect encouragement of colonial rebellions and the support of armed aggression by Russia's satellites. For their part, the capitalist powers were not slow to resort to propaganda aimed at combating communism, both within their own borders and within uncommitted states.

Any bargaining to be done between Russia and her former allies thus became tough. The bargaining strength of the Western Powers lay in the fact that America, and America only, had the atomic bomb. Russia, on the other hand, kept far greater numbers of men under arms. Furthermore, by its rapid advance westwards during the closing stages of the war, the Russian army had established a firm grip on eastern Europe. And when newly defeated Germany was parcelled out between Russia, Britain, America and France, Berlin—although it was itself divided between all four powers for purposes of occupation—fell within the Russian Zone.

It was over Berlin that the first big challenge of the Cold War arose. In 1948, in an attempt to oust the three Western Powers from their sectors of the city, the Russians mounted a land blockade of Berlin, cutting it off from the West. America and Britain responded with a massive airlift that lasted nearly 11 months, and succeeded in ferrying in more than 4,500,000 tons of supplies. In the end the Russians yielded and reopened the city's land communications.

The Berlin blockade was not the only disturbing incident of 1948. In the same year Europe had witnessed the take-over of Czechoslovakia by a communist government. So in 1949 the Western Powers set up the North Atlantic Treaty Organization (NATO), a combination of nine west European and North American countries, including Britain, the United States and Canada, which undertook to provide a NATO army on the continent as a bulwark against further communist expansion.

Yet whatever advantage the Western Powers may have gained by setting up NATO was jeopardized within a very few months, when it became known that Russia, too, now possessed the atomic bomb. This raised the spectre of atomic war between the opposing blocs, bringing wholesale devastation in its train. That spectre became even more haunting in November 1952, with a report that at Eniwetok atoll in the mid-Pacific the United States had exploded a hydrogen bomb, vastly more destructive than the original atomic bomb. Ten months later the first Russian hydrogen bomb was exploded. Within a very few years Britain and France had joined the "nuclear club," and the two great super-powers were stock-piling not only hydrogen bombs but also intercontinental missiles with which to deliver them.

It was then well within the bounds of possibility that if the communist and anti-communist powers should ever go to war, each could lay waste most of the other's major cities and wipe out a substantial portion of its entire population within a matter of days. The only hope seemed to be that the very destructiveness of these weapons would act as a deterrent to war making.

To a large extent that hope has so far been realized. Since the advent of nuclear weapons none of the Western Powers has en-

Member nations of the North Atlantic Treaty Organization often co-operate in military exercises, and share many weapons in common. The photograph above shows a NATO firepower demonstration on Salisbury Plain, England, in 1975. The gun in the foreground is a 105 mm. Pack Howitzer manned by Belgian gunners. The second gun crew is British and the third Italian. The tank-like gun in the background is a 107 mm. Howitzer. On the left is the standard F.N. 7.62 mm. self-loading rifle, fitted with a magazine holding 20 shots. This rifle is frequently modified to meet the needs of individual nations.

gaged in direct armed conflict with Russia or other east European communist countries; no big wars have been fought on the mainlands of Europe, the Americas or Australasia; and the world as a whole has been spared the horrors of a nuclear holocaust. Yet in Asia and Africa there have been many wars, including a few fought on a very considerable scale; and in nearly all of them can be seen the hand of communism, either exploiting the natural desire of colonial peoples for independence or supporting the aggression of a communist satellite.

Among the peoples of Asia, especially, the desire for independence was strongly spiced with hope when the Second World War ended. They remembered the seeming ease with which Japan had seized vast Asian "possessions" from Britain, France, Holland and the United States in 1942. It was true that the Japanese had now been driven out. But were the colonial powers quite as strong as they had once appeared to be, especially now that they themselves had suffered the ravages of war? Was not the time now ripe to throw off colonial rule altogether? And would not the communist countries—ideologically opposed to colonialism and to the colonial powers—lend moral and possibly material support to those who made the attempt?

The Indian subcontinent managed to achieve independence without resorting to war and without external aid. There, campaigns for self-government were bedevilled by hostility between

Top of page: A United States field
artillery battalion in action in Korea
in October 1951. Above: North Korean
prisoners, photographed in late autumn
1950. The fleece-lined caps and quilted
uniforms they wear are an indication
of the bitter weather conditions.

Left: Map showing the steady increase
in communist control of east Asia from
1938 to 1974. Since the Second World
War ended, communist and non-
communist powers have been involved
in three wars of considerable magnitude
in this region, one in Korea and two in
Vietnam. In addition, Britain had to wage
a long campaign to wear down communist jungle fighters in Malaya before
negotiating that country's independence.

Hindus and Moslems, which throughout 1946 resulted in serious
rioting. After negotiating the setting-up of two separate independent states—India mainly Hindu and Pakistan mainly
Moslem—Britain therefore withdrew in 1947, largely to avoid a
head-on collision with either of the two great religious communities. But in Indo-China, Indonesia, Malaya and Korea
events took a very different course.

In 1946 the French, attempting to regain their possessions in
Indo-China, came into conflict with the Viet Minh nationalists who, under the communist leader Ho Chi Minh, had earlier
declared Vietnam (part of Indo-China) to be an independent
republic. Eight years of bitter fighting—much of it guerrilla
fighting—followed, and in the course of it another Vietnamese
leader emerged, the non-communist Bao Dai. He, unlike Ho
Chi Minh, was prepared to accept the independence of Vietnam
within a French union. In 1949 the kind of state he accepted was
set up in the southern part of the country, with Saigon as its
capital, and this new state received French recognition. The
struggle was then between France and the south on the one hand
and the Viet Minh forces in the north on the other. Russia and
China gave military aid to the north while the United States
gave similar aid to the south.

The fighting culminated in May 1954, when the French
garrison in the fortress of Dien Bien Phu was forced to surrender
after a two-month siege. Vietnam was then divided into two
zones, communist North Vietnam and non-communist South
Vietnam, separated by the 17th parallel.

In the East Indies the Dutch were no more successful in re-
gaining their Asian possessions than were the French. There an

independent Republic of Indonesia was declared less than a week after the Japanese surrender. Dutch troops—and, at first, British troops too—fought sporadically against the Indonesian People's Army until December 1948. Then the United Nations Security Council called for immediate cessation of hostilities. A year later Indonesia gained formal recognition of its independence. Only for a very short time, in the autumn of 1948, was there any marked communist activity, when a local communist leader attempted to set up a "soviet government" in Java; and it was the Indonesians themselves who ousted him.

Britain, trying to re-establish her sovereignty in Malaya, came up against far more determined communist opposition—and met it with marked success. There communist guerrillas, drawn mainly from the Chinese section of the population, tried to gain control of the peninsula by making unceasing jungle raids on British troops and by terrorizing peaceful citizens into co-operating with them. But the British force included many professional soldiers trained in jungle warfare and capable of living in the jungle for weeks at a time without requiring more than occasional airborne supplies. In 12 years of almost purely infantry fighting, from 1948 to 1960, the guerrillas lost twice as many men as the British and were slowly but surely worn down. Malaya was eventually granted the independence that the guerrillas had been unable to seize at gunpoint for their own political ends.

The Korean War was quite a different matter. It was an example not of a national rebellion but of armed aggression by a communist satellite. And to appreciate the problems it raised, one has to remember that by 1949 the whole of mainland China had been brought under communist control and Mao Tse-tung had proclaimed the People's Republic of China. Thus there were now two major communist powers in the world, China and Russia. The former shared a long frontier with North Korea, and the latter had ports and a powerful naval base—Vladivostok—only a few miles away.

In June 1950, when the Russian-trained North Korean army invaded South Korea, whose troops had been trained by the United States, UNO took swift action and rushed American troops from Japan to Korea. The Americans were reinforced by contingents from other UN members, including British troops. On the other side, China intervened by sending in "volunteers" when the UN forces neared the Yalu river—the frontier between North Korea and Manchuria—late in the year.

Though technically a limited conflict, taking place only within the frontiers of Korea, the Korean War had serious implications as a confrontation between the communist and non-communist worlds. For the United Nations this was a difficult war to fight. First, America's President Truman declared Chinese territory out of bounds for land or air attack, for fear that the war might escalate into a world conflict. Next, in Korea's rugged and mountainous terrain, the technical superiority of the UN forces counted for little. This was no country for tanks, and without the full advantage of such mechanized weaponry the UN troops had

Below: One of the half a million American soldiers who served in Vietnam. Armed with an M16 rifle, he carries a smoke grenade on his shoulder strap and a deadly Claymore anti-personnel mine in the bag on his left hip.

Left: A helicopter brings reinforcements
to a Vietnamese battlefield.
Helicopters first came into their own
for military use in Korea, in the early
1950s. By the mid 1960s they were
much bigger and far more extensively
used. Some of them were heavily armed.

Below: Not all Viet Cong weapons were
supplied by China and North Vietnam.
Many were the spoils of war. This man,
with rice bag slung around his shoulders,
carries a MAT 49 collapsible rifle—
a legacy from the Viet Minh, who captured it years earlier from the French.

to fight—in a manner more reminiscent of the First World War
than the Second—against massed Chinese infantry attacks, fed
from China's inexhaustible supply of manpower. So hostilities
dragged on for three years before a final armistice was signed.
Territorially there was no winner and no loser. The boundary
between North and South Korea remained virtually unchanged.

The biggest, longest, bloodiest and most costly war of recent
times was the second war in Vietnam. The North Vietnamese never wholeheartedly accepted the division of the
country decided on in 1954. Within three years communist
guerrillas from the north (the Viet Cong) began penetrating the
rural areas of the south; and by 1960 South Vietnam, whose
troops were as yet only partially trained—by French and United
States officers—was in grave danger of losing control of much of
its territory. Late in 1961, therefore, the United States sent helicopter units to support the South Vietnamese army. Thereafter
American involvement increased until at one stage almost half a
million American soldiers were fighting in Vietnam, most of
them being conscripts, serving for comparatively short periods.
They were up against dedicated Viet Cong guerrillas, thoroughly
habituated to jungle warfare and fighting on their home ground;
they were also up against the now highly trained official army of
North Vietnam, which was eventually well equipped with tanks
and Russian artillery pieces. And although the Americans and
South Vietnamese had a formidable array of air power and highly
advanced weapons, they found that this was ultimately of no
avail against a lightly armed enemy operating with great skill in

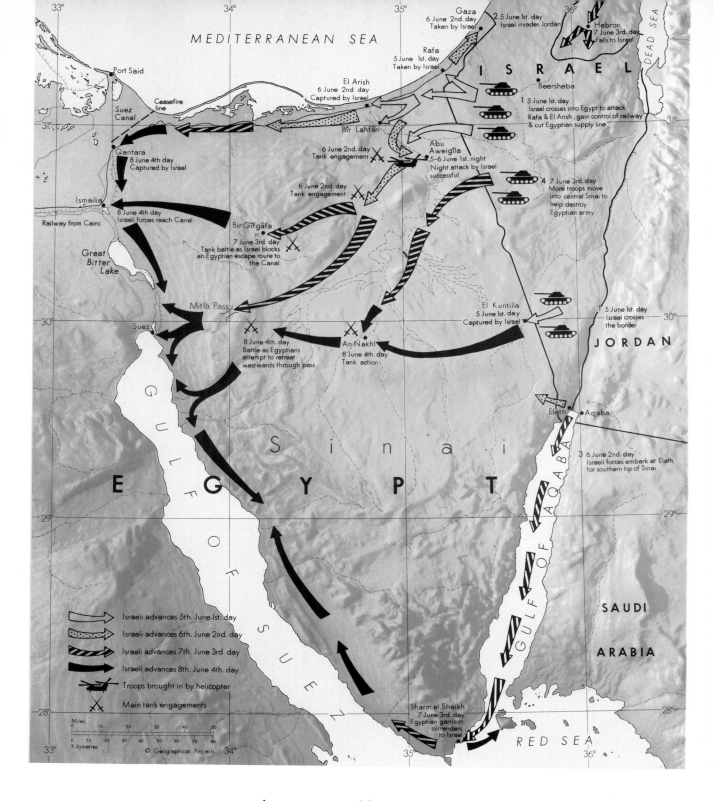

Map labels:

MEDITERRANEAN SEA

DEAD SEA

Gaza
6 June 2nd. day
Taken by Israel

2 5 June 1st. day
Israel invades Jordan

Hebron
7 June 3rd. day
Falls to Israel

I S R A E L

Rafa
5 June 1st. day
Taken by Israel

El Arish
6 June 2nd. day
Captured by Israel

Port Said

Beersheba

Ceasefire line

Suez Canal

Bîr Lahfân

1 5 June 1st. day
Israel crosses into Egypt to attack
Rafa & El Arish, gain control of railway
& cut Egyptian supply line

Qantara
8 June 4th. day
Captured by Israel

6 June 2nd. day
Tank engagement

Abu Aweigîla
5–6 June 1st. night
Night attack by Israel
successful

Ismailia

6 June 2nd. day
Tank engagement

4 7 June 3rd. day
More troops move
into central Sinai to
help destroy
Egyptian army

8 June 4th. day
Israeli forces reach Canal

Railway from Cairo

Bir Gîfgâfa

7 June 3rd. day
Tank battle as Israel blocks
an Egyptian escape route to
the Canal

Great Bitter Lake

Mitla Pass

El Kuntilla
5 June 1st. day
Captured by Israel

1 5 June 1st. day
Israel crosses
the border

Suez

8 June 4th. day
Battle as Egyptians
attempt to retreat
westwards through pass

An Nakhl
8 June 4th. day
Tank action

J O R D A N

G U L F   O F   S U E Z

S i n a i

Elath   Aqaba

3 6 June 2nd. day
Israeli forces embark at Elath
for southern tip of Sinai

E G Y P T

G U L F   O F   A Q A B A

SAUDI

ARABIA

Legend:

Israeli advances 5th. June 1st. day
Israeli advances 6th. June 2nd. day
Israeli advances 7th. June 3rd. day
Israeli advances 8th. June 4th. day
Troops brought in by helicopter
Main tank engagements

Miles
0 10 20 30 40 50
0 10 20 30 40 50 60 70 80
Kilometres
© Geographical Projects

Sharm el Sheikh
7 June 3rd. day
Egyptian garrison
surrenders
to Israel

RED SEA

---

the swamps and jungles of Vietnam. In 1973, America withdrew without victory, and two years later South Vietnam fell to the last great communist push.

Since the Second World War, the demand for an end to colonial rule has been just as widespread in Africa as in Asia. But in general the demand began somewhat later in Africa than in Asia and met with less resistance from the colonial powers, several of which had by then begun to doubt whether colonial rule could be morally justified. The first considerable territory to gain independence, in December 1951, was Libya, formerly an Italian colony. In January 1954 the Sudan, formerly under joint

Above: An Israeli tank advancing into Syria during the Yom Kippur War, 1973. The Israeli soldiers protect their ears from the deafening roar of their guns.

Left: Map showing some of the main events of the Six Day War (June 5 to June 10, 1967). In the first four days, the Israelis captured the whole of the Sinai peninsula from Egypt—an area far larger than their own country. In the course of the same brief war, they also occupied all Jordanian territory to the west of the Jordan and made small gains in southern Syria.

Egyptian-British rule, became self-governing. In 1957 it was followed by Ghana, formerly the Gold Coast, under British rule, and in 1958 by the Republic of Guinea, formerly part of French West Africa. And in a single month—July 1960—nearly a dozen more independent African states emerged, including the Somali Republic, the Ivory Coast, Dahomey, Niger and Chad.

Most of these states gained their independence with little or no bloodshed, but in later years several other African colonies resorted to violence, or even to open war, before they became self-governing. Among them were the Belgian Congo, where fighting grew so fierce that UNO had to send in troops before the independent state of Zaïre eventually came into being; Algeria, where French colonists took up arms against the mother country; and Kenya, where the Mau Mau employed violence and terrorism against British nationals. In these and other recent wars in Africa the main activity has again been guerrilla fighting.

It is probably true that of all the recent wars fought in Africa, eastern Asia and southeast Asia, only two have seriously threatened the peace of the entire world—the Korean War and the second war in Vietnam. But there is one especially sensitive region where almost any conflict can easily do so—western Asia, with its vast natural reserves of oil, so desperately needed in our energy-hungry world. And there, since the state of Israel came into existence in 1948, no fewer than six wars have been fought between Israel and her Arab neighbours, with Russia usually giving moral support and supplying arms to Arab countries and the United States usually doing the same for Israel.

At least two of these wars—the Six Day War of 1967, in which Israel occupied large Egyptian and Jordanian territories, and

the Yom Kippur War of 1973, in which neither side could gain a clear-cut victory—saw the use of highly sophisticated Russian and American weapons, almost as if the two super-powers were trying out their latest advances in war making technology by proxy. Yet paradoxically, both super-powers, fully alert to the dangers of war in this region, were quick to exert pressure on the belligerents to agree to a cease-fire; and both have since engaged in tireless diplomacy to lessen tension.

This is not the only paradox of war in the modern world. The Korean War and, to an even greater extent, the second war in Vietnam, revealed another: that even the highest degree of mechanization and the most sophisticated of modern weapons can offer no absolute guarantee of success against an ideologically inspired people fighting on its own ground. Thus although technological ingenuity has equipped armies with helicopters, vertical take-off planes, ultrasonic planes, sensors, detectors, rocket missiles that home unerringly on targets, memory-storage computers to perfect the accuracy of artillery fire and countless other modern devices, it may well be that the real war-winners are of a quite different kind. Against the lightly armed guerrilla, living roughly and fighting toughly in his native countryside, all the evidence suggests that the opponent most likely to prevail is the foot soldier, armed equally lightly, living equally roughly, fighting equally toughly and getting to know the countryside equally well—in fact, becoming basically a guerrilla fighter himself. And against a state prepared to resort to brain-washing to undermine resistance to the acceptance of its ideology, perhaps the only sure defence is the soldier who adheres no less firmly to an alternative ideology.

The advent of nuclear weapons has so far acted as a deterrent to the waging of nuclear war. But this map shows that since 1939 wars fought with conventional weapons have troubled almost every part of the world. The human race still has far to go to achieve the ideal of world peace and security.

122

IRELAND
1968–
conflicts

BERLIN BLOCKADE
1948

Riots at Gdansk & other ports
1970

INVASION OF CZECHOSLOVAKIA
1968
U.S.S.R. v. Czechoslovakia

HUNGARIAN UPRISING
1956

GREEK CIVIL WAR
1944–45
1967
Coup by Army officers

1945–60, 1963–67, 1974–75
Greek v. Turkish Cypriots

1949–50
Afghanistan
v. Pakistan

1950
Communist China invades Tibet

KOREAN WAR
1950–53
North Korea v. South Korea

1954–62
France v. Algerian
slem nationalists

1957–61
France v.
Tunisian
nationalists

SUEZ CRISIS
1956
Israel, Britain &
France v. Egypt

A

JORDANIAN
CIVIL WAR
1970

1951
Iran occupies
Abadan, Britain
withdraws

KASHMIR DISPUTE
1947–50, 1965
India v. Pakistan

1971
West Pakistan v.
East Pakistan

1961
India v. Port. Goa,
Damao & Diu

INVASION OF INDIA
1962
Communist China v. India

1956
Communist China
invades Burma

1946–54
France v. Vietnam

1958
Communist China v. Nationalist China

VASION OF GUINEA
70
rt. Guinea v. Guinea

1966
Chad v. Sudan

YEMENI CIVIL WAR
1962–65

VIETNAMESE WAR
1954–74
North Vietnam v. South Vietnam

NIGERIAN CIVIL WAR
1967–70
Federal government v. Biafra

1964
Ethiopia v. Somalia

1948–60
Britain v. communist guerrillas

1963–67
Rwanda v. Burundi

MAU MAU INSURRECTION
1952–56
Terrorists v. white settlers

CIVIL WAR IN CONGO REP
1960–64
Government v. Katanga

A   WAR BETWEEEN ISRAEL & ARAB LEAGUE
1948
ARAB–ISRAELI WAR
1967
Israel v. Syria, Egypt & Jordan
YOM KIPPUR WAR
1973
Israel v. Egypt, Syria, Jordan, Morocco & Iraq

1946–49
Netherlands v.
Indonesians

CIVIL WAR IN ANGOLA
1975–76

1949
France v.
nationalists

© Geographical Projects

But until the opening months of 1976 the most hopeful of all the paradoxes was that while the world's powers were still spending large proportions of their resources on producing incredibly devastating weapons, they were at the same time making genuine efforts to ease world tensions; and for a time the watchword everywhere was *détente*.

In January and February 1976, however, communist countries intervened in the affairs of newly independent Angola, ensuring its ultimate control by the left-wing **MPLA** faction, thus arousing fears of similar intervention in Rhodesia and South Africa. As a result, many Western politicians are now saying that for the future verbal protestations of peaceful intentions are not enough. The genuineness of all peace making efforts, from whatever quarter, must be judged by deeds rather than words.

Index

References in *italics* are to captions to pictures or maps.

Acknowledgments

Page 3 Rotunda Museum of Artillery/Photo Eileen Tweedy © Aldus Books: Page 13 (L) Reproduced by permission of the Trustees of the British Museum: 13 (C) Courtesy of the Oriental Institute, University of Chicago: Page 13 (R) By courtesy of the Israel Department of Antiquities and Museums, exhibited in the Israel Museum, Jerusalem: Pages 14-15 (T) Michael Holford photo: Pages 14-15 (B) Reproduced by permission of the Trustees of the British Museum: Page 16 (T) Cairo Museum/Photo Roger Wood: Page 19 (T) British Museum/Michael Holford photo: Page 19 (B) British Museum/Photo Roger Hyde © Aldus Books: Pages 28 (B), 29 (R) The Mansell Collection, London: Page 30 Josephine Powell, Rome: Page 31 Aubrey Singer/B.B.C./Robert Harding Associates: Page 34 (B) Biblioteca Nacional, Madrid/Mas: Page 36 The Mansell Collection, London: Page 37 (B) Published by permission of the Danish National Museum: Page 39 Michael Holford photo: Page 40 (T) The Armouries, Tower of London/Photo Derek Witty © Aldus Books: Page 43 (B) Edinburgh University Library: Page 46 (TL) The Governing Body of Christ Church, Oxford: Page 46 (BL) Antikvarisk-Topografiska Arkivet (ATA), Stockholm/Photo Sören Hallgren, 1976: Pages 46-7 (T) British Library Board: Page 47 (B) The Tower of London/Photo Derek Witty © Aldus Books: Page 50 (T) Rotunda Museum of Artillery/Photo Eileen Tweedy © Aldus Books: Page 50 (C) (B) The Tower of London/Photos Derek Witty © Aldus Books: Page 51 (T) (C) Marilyn Hunt © Aldus Books: Page 51 (B) Prints Division, The New York Public Library, Astor, Lenox and Tilden Foundations: Page 53 Archives Photographiques, Paris: Page 54 (CR) Rotunda Museum of Artillery/Photo Eileen Tweedy © Aldus Books: Page 55 Blenheim Tapestry, Green Writing Room, Blenheim Palace/His Grace the Duke of Marlborough: Page 60 (TL) British Crown Copyright. Science Museum, London: Page 62 (TL) Wellington Museum/Photo Eileen Tweedy © Aldus Books: Page 64 Rotunda Museum of Artillery/Photo Eileen Tweedy © Aldus Books: Page 65 (T) Marilyn Hunt © Aldus Books: Page 65 (B) Imperial War Museum, London: Page 66 (B) Bildarchiv Preussischer Kulturbesitz, Berlin: Page 74 (T) (B) Radio Times Hulton Picture Library: Pages 74-5 (C) Gettysburg National Military Park/Photo The Lane Studio © George Rainbird Ltd.: Page 76 The Library of Congress: Page 77 Rotunda Museum of Artillery/Photo Eileen Tweedy © Aldus Books: Pages 80-1 (T) B.B.C. Press Publicity photo: Pages 80-1 (B) Robert Hunt Library: Pages 84-5 (C) Imperial War Museum, London: Page 85 (R) Rotunda Museum of Artillery/Photo Eileen Tweedy © Aldus Books: Page 87 (B) Popperfoto: Pages 88 (T), 90-1, 92-3 (B) Imperial War Museum, London: Page 95 (B) Marilyn Hunt © Aldus Books: Pages 98-9 (B) Rotunda Museum of Artillery/Photo Eileen Tweedy © Aldus Books: Page 99 (T) Imperial War Museum, London: Page 101 (T) Ullstein GMBH Bilderdienst: Pages 102 (TR), 104 (T), 105, 106 (B), 107 (TL) Imperial War Museum, London: Pages 110-11 (C) United Kingdom Atomic Energy Authority: Pages 114-15 Soldier Magazine: Page 117 U.S. Army photos: Pages 119 (TL), 121 Popperfoto